ESCAPE FROM
DEBT

ESCAPE FROM DEBT

MAKE A PLAN
TAKE ACTION
GET HAPPY
& LOVE YOUR LIFE!

TIM WILLIAMSON

Wrightbooks

Also by Tim Williamson

Escape from Smoking

First published 2010 by Wrightbooks
an imprint of John Wiley & Sons Australia, Ltd
42 McDougall Street, Milton Qld 4064

Office also in Melbourne

Typeset in Berkeley LT 12/15.4pt

© Tim Williamson 2010

The moral rights of the author have been asserted

National Library of Australia Cataloguing-in-Publication entry:

Author:	Williamson, Tim (Timothy Andrew), 1974–
Title:	Escape from debt: make a plan, take action, get happy and love your life! / Tim Williamson.
ISBN:	9781742469584 (pbk.)
Notes:	Includes index.
Subjects:	Debt. Finance, Personal.
Dewey Number:	332.02402

Cover design by Xou Creative

Cover image © iStockphoto.com/gabyjalbert

Printed in Australia by McPherson's Printing Group

10 9 8 7 6 5 4 3 2 1

Disclaimer
The material in this publication is of the nature of general comment only, and does not represent professional advice. It is not intended to provide specific guidance for particular circumstances and it should not be relied on as the basis for any decision to take action or not take action on any matter which it covers. Readers should obtain professional advice where appropriate, before making any such decision. To the maximum extent permitted by law, the author and publisher disclaim all responsibility and liability to any person, arising directly or indirectly from any person taking or not taking action based upon the information in this publication.

Contents

About the author

Tim has flown as a commercial pilot in three countries. He is an experienced business owner, fitness coach, martial arts instructor and masseur with a passion for health, fitness and teaching.

A car accident in 2002 saw him grounded from flying and unable to continue fitness coaching, so he has since studied many different areas of business and personal development. He is a former bank employee and debt collector.

Acknowledgements

I would like to thank my partner, Nicole, for her wonderful support. I would also like to express my gratitude to the great team at John Wiley & Sons, Australia, and to you, the reader.

Introduction

Whether you have a lot of debt or just a little, I'm going to show you what it means to your cash flow and, ultimately, to your life, to have unnecessary drains on your finances. I'm going to give you the tools you need to free yourself. By understanding how the world of finance works, the marketing and human behaviour, not only will you be able to escape from debt and start living the life you want, but you will be able to help others do the same.

As much as we might like to, there is no way that we can make debt disappear. The only way out is to create a payment plan and follow it with discipline and dedication.

What you need to know is that this journey will be enlightening and enjoyable. Unlike a lot of finance books this one is written with a view towards human nature and breaking destructive patterns of behaviour, rather than facts and figures.

The process of lending money is nothing new and the expectation of being reimbursed for taking that risk is inherent. Credit is a tool of leverage. It can help you to buy your own home or have something now that would normally take years to save up for. There is nothing wrong with using credit, but there is everything wrong with going so far that you can't afford to make the repayments or you have to spend all your time working in order to service the account. Debt can make you a slave to a system that loves to profit from your efforts.

Talking about finances is something that does not come easily to a lot of people, and by the time people come to me for guidance they are defeated. In terms of motivation and regaining a foothold, this can mean that there is going to be some work required when it comes to your personal beliefs and your skills in resetting your focus and goals.

You have displayed the courage needed to take the initial step to escape from debt by reading this book, so well done. I will work with you to re-create your personal direction and rebuild your financial power. I'm going to show you where to start, how to create your plan of action and, most importantly, how to take action.

Recently there has been an increase in the number of people in financial strife. While it was predicted to happen by many finance writers and forecasters, no-one in the world was really prepared for the events of 2008. The impact of the global financial crisis (GFC), as it became known, took the world by surprise. The collapse of one financial giant after another saw systems weaken and people lose fortunes.

The GFC illustrated perfectly what the excessive and/or incorrect use of debt can do and the ramifications of leveraging one's finances heavily. The rise and rise of economies saw more companies and people investing in property and shares that were on a meteoric rise. But, as Sir Isaac Newton observed, what goes up must come down—and come down it did.

When the financial giants realised what was happening in the markets they called in their loans to their customers, who tended to be asset rich and heavily leveraged by debt. Companies and individuals sold their portfolios to liquidate their assets, but values fell too quickly. The assets were soon worth only half of what people had paid for them just a week earlier. The markets were in freefall and anyone who had been dependent on credit found themselves staring down the barrel of the GFC gun.

As companies began collapsing people's jobs disappeared and with it went their ability to maintain their lifestyles. As a result, stories of people losing their retirement funds or their houses, and relationships failing due to the stress from financial problems have become increasingly common.

Australians and New Zealanders are now spending an average 114 per cent of their income. With interest rates at their lowest levels in decades the temptation is there to increase debt levels to purchase houses and cars, but what will happen when interest rates increase?

In an exciting age of continuous change and development it is unfortunate that many people can't enjoy it due to their financial commitments. Much of the population is no longer working for themselves or their families, instead they are working to support interest payments. Using excess debt to fund your lifestyle is like sitting in a bath without a plug. You can turn the tap on and water comes out, but it goes straight down the drain. You can't lie back and relax because you are too busy worrying about the water flowing out. The amount you pay in interest and fees when you borrow money takes away from your hard-earned income, which means you have less to use. Your cash is going down the drain instead of you being able to enjoy it.

Once you put a plug in the bathtub, it begins to fill up. It's the same with debt—when you take control of your finances and start reducing your debts you will see how different life can be. You will discover a new and much more exciting side, a more comfortable and relaxing side. If you are stressed about money and feel as though you can't earn enough to get by, you will soon see that you can transform and create the life that you desire.

A number of years ago I was suffering under the weight of a great deal of debt. I had negatively leveraged my personal finances in order to have a nice car and the latest household gadgets. When I freed myself from debt I discovered that life did not have to be bought on credit. I didn't need to go to a financial institution with my hat in my hand to ask for more. I realised that I could put the cash I earned to better use by managing my impulses and complusions. I became aware that I could even make money through investing.

I will show you how to regain control of your cash flow and leverage the potential financial power you have. Today is your day to escape from debt.

The time is now

Throughout my life I have found that time is how I perceive it. If I concentrate on the ticking of a clock, then time will only move one second at a time. However, if I'm focused on a task that I enjoy, then time seems to move relatively quickly. Time is not a thing or something that happens. It is simply a means of how we each measure segments of our lives.

History is important because we can look back and glean the lessons from many situations. Understanding the past gives us the ability to learn and adjust for the future. But what about now? A concept I believe a lot of people find difficult to define is what *now* means to them.

By the time you have read this your *now* may be in the past or it may still be happening, so is now 'now' or is now … 'now'?

Confused yet? I'm not trying to complicate things, but just show you that *your time is how you consciously perceive it and how you make the best use of it.*

Life is a ceaseless dance and exchange of energy—it is fluid—so how do we embrace or take control of it? How can we make it work for us instead of just getting caught up in the flow? How can we make the most of our lives and avoid the feeling of being stuck or stagnant?

Recently I was woken in the middle of the night with a vexing question. People say to 'live for now', but what is now and what does it mean to you?

Is now the split second it takes to realise the instant you are in?

Is now five minutes?

Is now 10 hours?

Is now six months?

Is now 80 years?

Is now just the time it takes for our conscious mind to break free from the subconscious routines of day-to-day life to look around and smell the roses?

My point here is to open your conscious mind to the concept of 'now', take a strong hold of your life and make the decision to be in control and enjoy every aspect. You can even enjoy the truly challenging times by valuing the lessons they have to teach.

This brings me to another question: what is the definition of living to you?

Are you able to enjoy your life when you are overly stressed or worried about car payments, credit cards, mortgages and everything in between?

A lot of people wait for a time like New Year's Eve to make changes in their life. The problem is that it only comes once a year. The start of a new calendar year is seen as a chance to make a new beginning, and it is, but what about all the other 360-plus chances. No matter what is happening in your life or how busy you are, there is no better time than right now to start making the changes that you need to get ahead.

Is now your time?

Is the time right to escape from debt?

Absolutely!

Consciously take hold of 'now' with both hands and hold on tight. Here we go.

Instructions

You will notice that this book does not contain a lot of figures or statistics. I believe in showing you the principles behind the use of finance products and helping you to become proficient in their language and use. By understanding the fundamentals you will be able to change your financial behaviour and get on the road to reducing your debts. Everyone is in a different position financially, so to cite particular examples or case studies can make it difficult to include everyone. Instead, I will highlight the behaviours and beliefs behind the common mistakes, so you can draw a comparison with how you are operating.

There are just a few things I will ask you to do as you work with me on this program:

1   Dedicate some time right now to participate in this program. It will take you about three hours to read through and complete the exercises. It is my desire for you to read to the end without getting bored or confused by pages of figures and calculations, so I've made it easy to read without loads of jargon.

2   Have a glass of cold water with you. Coffee, tea, soft drinks, cordial and energy drinks are not going to help you concentrate as they all contain stimulants, which will give you unnatural highs and lows.

3   Don't be distracted. To ensure that you get the best from this program you will need to turn off your telephone and anything in the background that may disturb you, and hang a 'Do not disturb' sign on your door. You're going to need to completely immerse yourself for the next three hours.

4   Participate fully. A number of questions and
     exercises have been included in this book. Get a
     pen and write your responses in the blank space
     provided to cement in your mind the concepts
     that are presented. By writing your answers down
     you will find that the information becomes more
     'real' to you and you will retain more than you
     would if you just read through the pages. In fact
     your memory retention will be improved by up to
     80 per cent.

With the right momentum and guidance you will notice
that the money you save and the changes you make in
your life will create some incredibly powerful directions
for you to travel.

As a quick measure now I'd like to check your commitment to this program and the results you desire.

On a scale of 1 to 10, how strongly do you feel that you
honestly want to get out of debt right now? Circle your
answer.

0   1   2   3   4   5   6   7   8   9   10

Low desire   Strong desire

For this program to be completely effective, where do
you think your level of commitment and desire to get out
of debt has to be?

0   1   2   3   4   5   6   7   8   9   10

Low desire   Strong desire

I'm the kind of person who likes to keep my books in pristine condition. If you're the same, you'll have to undergo a small paradigm shift to make this program work. The more you write in this book the better. Don't hold back! Your first task is to put your name on the front page. *Own this book and the words you write.*

Use a coloured pen so your words stand out when you look back over them. Your answers will also create a great baseline for you to come back to in the future. You can see exactly where you were and what you were thinking at the time. My main aim for you is to be in command of your own life. By reading your answers you can evaluate your progress and make any adjustments required to keep you on track.

By learning something new each day and making small changes to improve everything you do, you will find that you become more fulfilled. Getting rid of old baggage such as personal debt will allow you to get the most out of your life and have as much as you desire.

When I became free from debt I noticed that the immediate changes in my cash flow meant that I could enjoy my down time. I became more aware of the world around me and I realised how controlled I was by the need to make a dollar. My new-found personal drive has promoted a true balance in my life, which gives me the ability to enjoy the good times, as well as comfortably deal with the normal challenges that life offers.

I want you to be able to live a life that is fulfilling and rich—emotionally, physically, mentally and financially. If you are constantly at work, worried about money, stressed or running low on energy, how can you feel complete and balanced? How can you positively contribute and 'give' to another person?

Changing your behaviour can take time and effort, and this book will be a solid companion as you work your way to freedom. There is no quick fix for anything, especially finance. Anyone who says otherwise is most likely going to cost you more money. You will have no doubt seen stories of people who have won the lottery, only to have lost it all within the space of a year, or people who have been on television weight-loss shows and have lost massive amounts of weight, but a year later have put most of it back on. Taking small steps and creating gradual change is the best way to move forwards; to adapt your mind and body to the new way of being.

Quick fixes and bandaid measures tend to be ineffective due to the lack of true guidance and learning opportunities. The quick fix often becomes a situation where responsibility takes a back seat or is handed to someone else altogether. Be sure to revisit this program on a regular basis and use it to monitor your progress.

Now you need to move forward but which way is that? Chapter 1 will help you find your direction.

Chapter 1

YOU HAVE TO KNOW WHERE YOU'RE GOING

How am I going to live today in order to create the tomorrow I'm committed to?

Tony Robbins

Before you commence a journey you need to know two things: where you are going and where to start. So, we need to find out where you stand financially. To do this you need to take some time now to fill in the budget overleaf to work out how much money is coming in each month and where it's all going—this is your current cash flow. By completing the budget you will have a clear picture of where you are right now—where you may be overspending, and where you can cut back and divert extra funds to paying off your debt. From that picture you will be able to create your plan to escape from debt.

Income	Monthly ($)
Wages or salary	
Investment income	
Interest earned	
Other income	
Total income	

Expenses	Monthly ($)
Rent or mortgage	
Household maintenance	
Home and contents insurance	
Electricity	
Gas	
Water	
Home phone	
Mobile phone	
Internet	
Groceries and takeaway meals	
Cigarettes and alcohol	
Child care and school fees	
Health insurance	
Medical expenses (doctor, dentist, specialists and so on)	
Car maintenance	
Car registration	
Car insurance	
Petrol and tolls	
Public transport	

Expenses	Monthly ($)
Taxis	
Credit card 1 repayment	
Credit card 2 repayment	
Credit card 3 repayment	
Store card repayment	
Personal loan repayment	
Interest-free account repayment (furniture, TV and so on)	
Lunches	
Dining out	
Hair and beauty treatments	
Entertainment	
Gifts	
Newspapers and magazines	
Memberships (club, gym and so on)	
Deposit into savings account	
Deposit into investments	
Other expenses	
Total expenses	

Total income – total expenses = _____

Are your expenses more or less than your income? Are you solvent (that is, are you able to pay all your accounts) or are you insolvent (that is, are you unable to pay all your accounts)?

....

....

If you were a business, would you be solvent and viable? If you were an investor, would you look at the previous figures and want to invest in yourself? If you are solvent, you should be able to see how much reserve cash you can use to reduce your liabilities. If you suspect you may be insolvent, read on to discover the steps you can take to begin changing that.

Now you know your starting point for this particular journey. The next stage is working out your destination and how you are going to get there. By understanding the marketing techniques credit providers use and the human behaviours and attitudes that the marketing invokes, you will be able to create a plan to avoid these behaviours and patterns. You will also learn about the common mistakes people make with their finances and how they can keep you locked into a system that enjoys receiving your money for nothing.

Where do you want to go?

A power that we all possess is the ability to dream, to imagine. Sometimes we get clouded over by our obligations and forget to use the part of the brain that allows us to be free and create our future. By creating mental pictures of where we want to be we can activate our brains to do something towards making that image a reality. We can use that image to assess whether what we are doing at that particular time is going to help us or hinder us.

All successful people and 'paths to success' books talk about goal setting, but what is it? Goal setting is simply defining what you would like to have happen in your life. It's the process of clarifying your direction.

Society at the moment could be pictured in the following way.

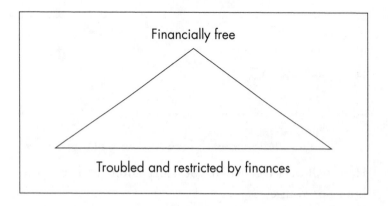

Mark where you think you are in this pyramid.

Right now you're probably like most adults who are working and paying off debts, and are struggling to move up from the base of the triangle.

Come back to this diagram in 12 months and draw another mark showing where you are at that point in time. It might be disheartening to think about a year of paying off debts, but take some time now to consider how you will feel if in two years from now you haven't made any changes and are still on the base of the pyramid. Imagine what your life will be like if you don't take action today.

What do you think you might miss out on in that time?

....

....

What do you think your life will be like in five years if you don't take action today?

....

....

How about in 10 years?

....

....

How will you feel when you can't afford to keep your house or your car?

....

....

Okay, shake out those painful images and breathe deeply. It's difficult to imagine how your life may be if you continue with your current damaging behaviour, but it is an important part of the process of moving forward. Today is your chance to make a better future for yourself. You can start making the changes you need to get ahead right now.

If you've made mistakes in the past that have led you to a position of financial trouble or hardship, you need to look back and forgive yourself for making those mistakes. The power of forgiveness will release the problem from your mind and it will become a position of learning and reflection instead. Forgiveness allows you to own a problem. There is no blame, no putting the problem aside and hoping it will disappear, and there are no excuses. Holding onto a grudge or past hurt will only do more damage to the energy of your thoughts and the potential power of your future planning and abilities.

Forgiveness is a great way to clear out and eliminate the SWC language (should have, would have, could have) from your life. The SWCs will keep you in a limited space in your mind, so get rid of them from your repertoire.

Do you need to forgive someone else for placing you in a difficult financial position?

What can you learn from any past mistakes?

....

....

How can you avoid making the same mistakes in the future?

....

....

Looking back on the past mistakes, what are you grateful for? Can you be grateful for the fact that they opened your eyes to a damaging behaviour or belief?

....

....

Now, think about where you would like to be in the pyramid. Make another mark in the diagram, this time in a different coloured pen.

Why do you want to get there?

....

....

What is your motivation?

....

....

It is one of my ultimate goals to help more people to gain the knowledge that can put them on the path to regaining control, and as such, see the trend of people in financial difficulty reversed, as shown in the following diagram.

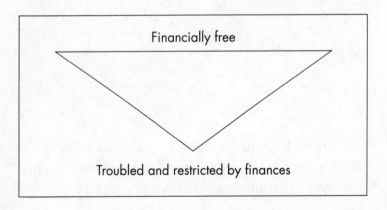

Financially free

Troubled and restricted by finances

This book is a financial freedom plan and there is some work involved, but I want you to have fun along the way. I'm going to introduce you to several strengths and abilities that we all have. The first is the power of your imagination. The second is the power to focus your thoughts and be clear about what you desire. The third is to take action and set foot on the road to success.

Using your imagination is not just about making pretty pictures in your mind. It is about creating images that are so real and so inspiring that they will cause you to feel the event as though it was actually happening, to feel inspired enough that you will want to take immediate action. The images you create will help remind you of your destination and keep your mind on the task at hand. They will cause your mind to believe that they are already real, already tangible.

By visualising where you want to be, you can ask questions to evaluate your progress. For example, 'Does buying this new flat-screen TV get me closer to or further away from my desired destination?'

Try this with me now. I want you to read this and the next paragraph, and then close your eyes and imagine. Picture yourself at a beautifully set table in a manicured garden where you are celebrating your freedom from debt with your friends.

What are you wearing? Is there laughter? Can you feel the sun warming your skin? Do you feel relaxed? Are you smiling? Take some time to create your scene and add a lot of detail to it. I want you to make that picture so real that you want to be there right now and you want to feel those feelings. Give your body and mind something to aim for.

This example is to show you that no matter what is happening in your life you can create a feeling of total relaxation and inner peace. The mental visualisation allows you to physically generate a slower heartbeat, muscular relaxation, deep diaphragmatic breathing and reduced blood pressure. From your mind you can contol your physical body.

In his 1905 findings Albert Einstein wrote the formula $E=mc^2$, which demonstrates the relationship between energy and matter. The formula shows that the two are interchangeable, and therefore that you can take the energy of your thoughts and feelings and convert them to matter — that is, they can become 'real' in your life.

I could write pages of instructions explaining how you can perform an action so you will get a result, and there are many good instruction manuals out there. Instead I want you to highlight why you want to escape from debt. I want you to create some momentum and become excited about what you are going to gain by making some changes to the way you handle your finances. By being clear about what you desire in your life and by generating a feeling of true excitement about the results, about being debt free, you'll actually create your own plans and follow them through.

For example, you might realise, like I did years ago, that your car is keeping you in debt. I had to go to work simply to make the repayments, and if I didn't go to work my car would be repossessed. This was a stressful time in my life, but the answer came that I should sell the car. I could still get around in a cheaper car, and while I didn't look like the most successful person on the road, as I drove around I saw people in expensive vehicles who weren't smiling. They had furrowed brows or were shaking their fists at other drivers.

This brings me to the question, why do you want to become debt free? List now how you will benefit in the following areas if you free yourself of unnecessary costs, interest payments and fees.

Happiness and wellbeing

....

....

Relationships and family life

....

....

Work life

....

....

Health and stress levels

....

....

Ability to invest or take advantage of opportunities

....

....

By reinforcing the positive direction you wish to take, you will find that you will attract the things that you desire. If your focus is on managing your finances and getting out of debt, you will discover that having made debt your focus you are actually attracting more of it into your life.

You need to change your language from 'I want to get out of debt' to 'I'm looking forward to enjoying the time created through effective financial management'. Say the following sentence out loud: 'I know that if I work my finances intelligently, I can have more fun, happiness, love and everything else I desire in my life'. Do you believe yourself?

Goal setting

If a goal is a definition of what you want to have happen in your life, what can you do to make it real to you?

To begin with, you have to know what you want. This in itself can be a challenge for a lot of people who have been living in a cloud of work and bills for so long. The great thing about goal setting and clear thinking is that it lifts the fog of day-to-day thoughts. These thoughts— of preparing dinner, washing clothes, feeding the pets, completing homework and so on—can cause you to lose focus on living and working towards your future, unless you incorporate them. Is there a way you can make daily activities enjoyable?

Asking a question or voicing your desire is a great way to open the door in your mind for the answer to come. I imagine the human mind is like a massive building with many rooms and doors. Starting out in the lobby as a child your parents or guardians open the doors for you. Your teachers at school open more doors, and as you grow older and gain experience and self-confidence you begin to open doors for yourself. Opening a door may just lead to a new room that is full of options for where you can go in life. Life is all about experiences and learning.

You will find that your instincts will draw you to certain paths, and quite often when you are clear about your direction you will find what you desire behind the door or down the path you choose. If you are unclear about what you want, you will find that your life is full of misdirection and you are trying to open doors without any thought for what lies beyond. Some people can go their whole lives opening doors and going from room to room without ever really knowing what they desire or why.

There are other times when you will open a door and something unexpected will happen. You may have an experience that will set you back or hurt you. After my car accident in 2002 I was bitter and angry at the world, and I fell into a negative whirlwind of depressive behaviour. Today, however, I believe the accident may have happened for a reason. It has helped me to grow and be in the position I am right now, so that I can help people to create better lives for themselves.

Setting a clear direction will help you to travel the path that you desire. You'll find that doors may even automatically open for you as you approach them so that you remain on the correct path. Have you ever had something happen that seemed like you were in the right place at the right time? Have you ever had a series of events transpire that have led you down a path of success? Have you ever seemed to attract people or situations into your life that felt as though they were meant to be? Have you ever had something negative happen that turned out to be an opportunity?

Like an electromagnet we can attract into our lives the things that we desire and repel those that we do not. Or we can attract into our lives the very things that we do not desire and repel what we do desire. It is how we engage our brains to work and generate thoughts in the correct manner that will work for us or against us. What we tell ourselves and others can have a direct effect on our abilities and fortunes.

Our surroundings can influence the electromagnetic field that we produce within ourselves. Large shopping centres are a perfect example of where we can lose ourselves and our power. The bright lights, music, product placement and so on creates confusion in our minds. There is too much information to be able to process it all effectively, so we tend to buy things that we normally wouldn't. We lose the power of controlled and rational thought.

Using focused thought, visualisation, planning, evaluation and action we can build and attract monetary wealth, emotional wealth, happiness, love, courage, self-confidence and any number of things that we would like to have in our lives. We can create good times, but we can also create times of emotional devastation—it all depends on the power of our focus and whether or not we are attuned to receiving what we desire.

Can you find 'good' in a bad situation? Yes, you can simply choose to focus on what is good at that time. Today there are wars raging and natural disasters taking heavy tolls, yet we can still find hope, we can still find joy if we choose to. You can choose to focus on the negative side of your financial position, or you can choose to focus on the positive direction in which you can travel. This will affect the direction in which you will travel and which door you will open next.

By simply sharing a smile and a kind word with someone we can affect the way they feel and the way they will interact with others. The flow-on effect of this positivity can compound quickly. By choosing to switch on a positive focus and a positive field, you will attract people or situations that suit the state you are in. Likewise, the power of a negative field can spread like wildfire.

Einstein's theory of energy becoming matter highlights the potential that is within us all. We all have the potential for great things and to make decisions that will change our lives forever. At any time you can choose to move from a negative path to one that will empower you to create the changes you desire in life. Many great leaders in history have risen from positions of desperation or total failure. You can move from a path of debt and despair to one that will lead you to a life where money serves you and time is on your side. If that is where you feel you have been, then the choice of direction is in your hands today.

What are your goals?

By creating clear goals and a clear direction you will be telling your mind that the path you desire to travel on is different from the one that you have previously been on. Once your direction is clear and your motivation is there you will begin to see the answers that you need to make changes. If you have to take a step back in order to move forward, then that is a decision you will have to make after considering your options.

Your goals will become defined when you:

- write them down

- clarify them with lots of detail

- give yourself a time frame to achieve them

- make them realistic and achievable

- share them with others, make them real and be accountable for your actions

- review them on a regular basis—remind yourself of what you are working towards

- revise them as your life changes.

Remember to celebrate the goals you achieve. For the larger goals, celebrate each time you make it a step closer to the big picture. When you do reach a goal, be sure not to rest on your laurels—create some new goals and keep moving forward. Goal setting is not a one-time task. To keep yourself on track and focused you should review your goals often. Have fun with your future possibilities.

When you have written your goals down, say them out loud. See them and hear them. Involve as many senses as you can and make your goals as real as possible.

Close your eyes and picture yourself as though you have already achieved your goals and reached your desired destination.

How would you look?

What would you be wearing?

Where would you be?

Who is with you?

Why are they with you?

Give your inner pictures as much detail and colour as possible, because when you make them real in your mind they will be easier to achieve.

A goal is only a goal if you *want* to get there. Not if someone else wants you to get there or if you *have* to get there.

You have taken the first step by reading this book. That shows me that you have what it takes to start working on achieving your goals, dreams and desires.

It is now time to set out some realistic plans, work through them with your family and perhaps even involve your friends. You might be surprised to find out how strong you can become and how much you can learn by working as a team. Involving other people and working together is a great way to motivate each other and achieve your desired outcome.

Involving others also creates a level of accountability — that is, a level of responsibility for your words and actions — so be careful what you tell others you are planning to achieve, as they may expect to see some results.

Where you go when you get out of debt is your choice. There are many directions you can take.

How do you want to celebrate the day you become debt free?

....

....

By what date do you want to be debt free?

....

....

We've all made excuses for not doing something, but how much harder does it make the task when you keep putting it off? Get it out of the way now and spend more time doing what you enjoy. If you have been good at procrastinating in the past, there is no reason to give up such a talent, just put the procrastination off until later. Clear your mind for the good stuff in life.

What motivates you? What really fires you up?

....

....

What de-motivates you? What slows you down?

....

....

Knowing the answers to those questions can help you to either avoid certain actions or maintain what you are doing to steer yourself towards your desired result.

The following statements will help you get started with your goals.

Goal 1: I will get the bank working for me instead of working for the bank.

Goal 2: I will set up a comprehensive and accurate budget that I can stick to.

Goal 3: I will spend less money than I earn.

Goal 4: I will remember that my life is happening now, so I will take the time to enjoy every aspect of my journey.

What other goals can you come up with right now?

....

....

By what date do you want to have achieved them?

....

....

What would you like to improve in your life and by when do you want to see the improvement?

....

....

The great thing about goals is that they can always be improved on and changed. They aren't fixed in concrete. Like us, goals continue to grow and evolve. Defined goals keep you looking forward as you travel through life. They give you something to focus on. Once you get close to or achieve your goals, you can set new ones for even further ahead.

Work out which goals you want to achieve first. Prioritising them will provide a structure and from there a plan will develop for you to get out there and realise them. Write the date for when you would like to achieve each of your particular goals. This will give you a frame of reference for how you should be progressing.

In high school I was the type of student who would stay up all night to complete a project that was due the next day. I hadn't learnt how to prioritise tasks or set goals—the lessons were all around me, I just didn't recognise or adopt them. My approach has certainly changed since then.

Doing a little bit each day is far easier than cramming everything in at the last moment and just hoping for a good outcome. There are many distractions that take us away from our awareness of the world around us. It may seem easier at times to sit and watch television than to take action on something that needs your attention.

What action can you take today to get started on the right path to paying off your debts?

Having a direction and something concrete to work towards is great motivation to take some action and make it happen. We can spend all day being idle and running scenarios through our heads, which most of the time are the wrong scenarios. Some can be disempowering thoughts of revenge or retribution, while others can be thoughts of past events where we wished we had spoken or acted differently. These trains of thought can take a lot of time away from actually making plans and taking action. Instead, spend some time planning for a great outcome and enjoy the rewards when you arrive at the destination.

When driving a car you have to keep your gaze forward to see what is coming. It's the same with working towards a goal. Keeping your eyes on your goals will help you to drive over or around all of the obstacles that stand in your way. It will also enable you to see all the possibilities and opportunities that are coming your way.

When you are driving and you reach your destination, do you stop the car and never drive it again? Of course not, you simply set a new destination, jump back in your car and drive on to it.

Don't sweat the small stuff, and keep your sights set on your goals. If you're constantly looking in the rear-view mirror, you will miss most, if not all, of the opportunities. You may only see them when they have already passed you by.

Learn from the past but do not dwell too long on it because the past can consume you. You need to let go of old regrets and past failures. Let go of the 'should'ves', 'would'ves' and 'could'ves'. Trade them for what you can achieve today and in the future.

I recommend that you revise your goals on a regular basis, so they stay fresh and up to date. Problems can arise when someone reaches their goal and then sits back on their laurels. They figure that the work has been done so they can relax. This is the point at which a maintenance program should begin or a new goal should be made. Use the momentum you have built up to climb to greater heights.

The winds of life have a funny way of changing direction on us. If you're sailing a yacht and the wind changes, you can decide to keep the sails and set-up of your yacht the same and hope to go in the same direction, or you can make a few small changes to the set-up of the sails and steering so that you use the wind to your best ability.

Chapter 2

CHANGING YOUR FINANCIAL BEHAVIOUR

*Give a man a fish and you feed him for a day. Teach a
man to fish and you feed him for a lifetime.*

Chinese proverb

During my flying career I was taught to constantly monitor and evaluate the situation that was around me. There
are engine systems, electrical systems, navigation, radio
communication, internal communications and everything
else associated with getting the aircraft, passengers and
freight to their destination safely that must be checked,
crosschecked and monitored.

A single oversight or mistake in any of the areas of oper-
ation can begin a chain of events that can end in disaster.
This chain is called the accident chain.

The links in the chain form as the situation progresses. By understanding the systems and operations you can see where the links in the chain are being created. You will also be able to read the signals so that you will know where you are in your journey and whether you are on track or off track.

The chain will continue to form until the minute it breaks. Different links will contribute to the chain and these links will be made from different materials of varying thickness and quality. The links will keep adding to the chain until the integrity of one of the links gives way or the chain itself becomes too long to be able to retain its form. Disaster comes when the chain breaks. In an aircraft accident this can mean people get hurt.

If you analyse your financial position, you will notice that there are links forming in your accident chain that if left unchecked could send you into a financial spin.

Have you accepted an increase on your credit card limit recently?

Have you refinanced your house and consolidated your credit cards or personal loan onto that platform?

Do you find that you can't take a day off work to look after an ill family member because of your financial obligations?

These are all links in the chain.

Can you see your financial accident chain being formed and where it may be strained? Write down some of your links below.

....

....

Awareness of the chain itself can be curative. You may be at the start of the chain through certain beliefs or attitudes towards credit or your cash flow, or you may have developed a chain that is perhaps only a link or two from breaking point. Right now you can change that. By changing what you are doing and how you are managing your money, you can stop the chain forming and leave it behind. The new level of awareness you will achieve will be your chance to stop your chain from forming and change your life for the better.

Debt-use behaviour

Staying in debt and working with credit becomes normal behaviour when we do it for long enough. When something is familiar to us we get comfortable and from there it is easy to become complacent. However, I want to show you how working with the wrong sort of debt, or working with the right debt in the wrong way, is keeping you from the fun and exciting times in life.

Most people are following the same behavioural patterns in using credit cards and personal finance. Increasing levels of debt have become normal and many of us expect our debt levels to rise on a regular basis. We take 'advantage' of credit level increases when they come in the mail and may even refinance our debts to manage the increasing monthly repayment levels. My own levels of personal debt crept up to the point where I had no money left at the end of the month for my own use. I was working only to pay bills and had no time or energy left for anything or anyone. Familiarity does breed contempt and contempt can cost you everything.

Some time ago I attended a business course. The lecturer had run a haberdashery business and was versed in the day-to-day operations of a retail store. When it came to the topic of credit use, he told us that any offer of credit was good. If a business was to offer you 30 days to pay, why would you pay immediately? I have also heard financial commentators support this line of thinking. One ludicrous comment the lecturer made was that the account should be paid only when the debt collectors came calling. I have seen people take this sort of advice and then witnessed the negative effects on their family and friends.

There are a number of reasons I do not support the use of credit (unless it is for investment purposes), which are as follows:

- Unless you're dealing with many thousands of dollars, what good is the money in your bank account or pocket for an extra 30 days?

- If you consistently pay your accounts on time, the supplier will look more favourably on you should the need arise in the future. You can also wield more power when asking for discounts or allowances on your account status.

- You won't be stressed about your cash flow, or about receiving threatening letters or fees and charges, if you pay your bills as soon as they come in.

- You can operate to a budget and the figures will be relatively accurate and understandable. If you are running 30 days behind on one account and 60 days behind on another, it becomes difficult to correctly forecast your budget and control your cash flow.

- The extra distance you can create by paying bills before their due date will give you more breathing space should something unforeseen interrupt your plans and set you back.

- Just because other people are buying things on credit, why should you?

Banks and lending institutions have stood the test of time for a good reason; they turn a profit. It's a simple equation in business:

Good business = profit (businesses like to make money)

Profit = happy shareholders (shareholders like to make money)

In Australia, a country with a population of approximately 21 million, the banks make billions of dollars in profit.

While a lot of it is from business and investment accounts, much is also from people like you and me. Did you know that about half of the banks' yearly profits are from fees and charges alone? Do you know where your money is going?

Figures from the Reserve Bank of Australia show that we are now more than $1.2 trillion in debt. This equates to about $55000 per head of population, and includes home loans, credit cards and personal loans. With debt consolidation becoming an everyday occurrence, however, it is difficult to distinguish exact levels of personal debt.

New Zealanders are in debt to the tune of about $27000 per head of population, according to its Reserve Bank. And, according to Visa, with online spending in New Zealand increasing by 97 per cent in 2009, the country is hot on Australia's heels for increasing levels of personal debt.

It is the aim of every good business to make a profit, and it is now time for you to treat yourself as a business. The bank should be working for you — not the other way around. Stop surviving and start thriving!

For too many people life has become a continuous pattern of work, pay bills, sleep, work, pay bills, sleep. It's time to break free from that pattern. The people I speak with who have substantial investments do not use credit cards or personal loans to purchase what they have. They have harnessed the power of financial leverage and have made money work for them instead of against them.

I'll never denounce the financial institutions because they do allow ideas to be formed into reality. Indeed, many investment opportunities have been made possible using debt as a tool to create leverage. However, there is a problem with tools. Any professional tradesperson can tell you that using a power tool without the appropriate safety equipment and training can be extremely dangerous. It is common for people to lose hands, fingers, legs and even their lives through accidents and the misuse of power tools. Debt is the same. It can cripple you for life, or worse. The correct education will help you to avoid becoming a statistic.

There are many great wealth creation books out there and they all contain valuable information, but you may find it difficult to identify with them as they are generally directed at people who are starting from a different position. The holes in your finances have to be filled before you can take that next financial step.

Like a child who falls over while taking their first steps you will have the occasional fall and get some bumps and scratches. Just dust yourself off and learn from the experience. The key to success is to keep getting back on your feet and continuing on your journey.

There are companies that profess to manage your budget and finances, but handing your responsibility to someone else is not going to empower you for the future. It may seem like an easy fix for now, but it is highly likely the old problems will return.

Use this book as a starting point for your education, so you can look at your own finances and start making responsible decisions for what you want to have happen in your life. Take some positive steps forward.

Be prepared

When I was in Scouts we had a motto: 'Be prepared'.

Having wealth is something that needs to be planned and prepared for. Money can be controlled or it can be controlling, and it is essential to understand this distinction. If you want to be rich and successful, you need to think rich and successful thoughts, and then follow them up with rich and successful actions. The same goes if you desire love or happiness. To gain love in your life you need to think loving thoughts and act with love. When you do that you will need to be prepared to receive love in abundance. Being prepared means you will be less likely to squander your fortune when it comes along.

Have you ever had one of those days where nothing seems to go right? If you don't consciously stop the cycle and let your mind continue with the negative day, you can find that situations will get out of control very quickly, and instead of getting better they get worse. You fall into a pattern of thought that says, 'Oh no, today is just terrible! Everything is going wrong for me'. The focus of that thought is going to mean that nothing will go right and you will create situations where problems seem to arise from nowhere.

There is a downward spiralling tornado effect that sucks you in and drags you deeper into itself. Being aware of this tornado effect means you can step out of the whirlwind at any time and plateau or change direction. When you are caught up in the negative tornado, try to remember that in order to get on the upwards spiral you need to change your thought and behavioural patterns.

Similarly, if you wake up and feel terrific, you seem to find that those days are a breeze. Things just click into place and people respond positively to your upbeat energy. You feel more relaxed and the upwards spiral of each small success carries you even higher. Like a tornado your positive actions, language and emotions will carry you higher. If you're in the upward spiral, then you can plateau by deciding to quit while you are ahead. This instantly stops that upwards trend. Why would you want to quit when you're ahead? You can use the momentum you already have to go even higher.

On either pattern you can bring it back to a plateau and even reverse it by changing the pattern of your thoughts and behaviour. If you're caught in the negative tornado, take the time to stop for a moment and look for something to smile about. See if you can find humour in a situation or something that will help you to alter the negative pattern of behaviour and turn it around to serve you. What can you be grateful for?

Something you can change instantly is the way you speak to yourself, your inner monologue. Instead of saying something such as 'I'm hopeless at this, it will never work' say 'I have a problem with getting this happening. What can I change to make it work? How can I approach the problem so that it will be resolved easily? What can I learn from my mistakes so that I don't repeat them?'

Stop beating yourself up and give your brain something it can actually work with. Being grateful for a learning and personal growth opportunity can be a powerful way to turn the tornado in a positive direction.

Chapter 3

CAN YOU AFFORD THAT?

You have to decide what your highest priorities are and have the courage…to say 'no' to other things.

Steven Covey

When it comes to debt and buying something new it is quite common to go over the budget we set for ourselves. We have all done it, but it is my hope that after reading this book you will no longer spend what you can't afford.

A key point in modern sales training is for the sales-person to 'upsell' and 'value add'. This is something that companies such as McDonald's have become famous for. The question 'Would you like fries with that?' is one we've all heard. The upsell is an offer that requires an instant decision from the buyer. People are mostly trained to say 'yes', so it is the first answer that comes subconsciously, whether you want the fries or not. We don't want to offend the person asking the question or making the offer.

It is not rude or arrogant to say 'no' to someone. Salespeople are trained to turn excuses around, so if you say no, a good salesperson can still turn your excuse into a 'yes'.

People who sell cars, furniture, household goods and other items are always looking for ways to upsell. Questions I rarely hear from salespeople are, 'What is your budget?' or 'What can you afford?' The solution they have been trained to give hesitant buyers is that they can apply for finance (usually through the store, which means greater commissions for the salesperson or better profits for the store). Some will even falsify the sales documents and lie to your face if it means they will receive a better bonus or save their job. While this behaviour is extreme, it does exist, so the best way to move safely through the sales process is to know your limitations before you walk into the store. Doing some research and knowing what you want to buy is even better.

Unfortunately, although they may have a fair idea of what they can afford, it is the upsell and guessing the uppermost limits of their budget that places so many people in financial predicaments. In chapter 1 you filled in your budget, so you should be well aware of what you can afford.

Setting a budget will give you an idea of whether or not you can upgrade to the 'premium' package, which is usually only available to a select few (everyone) or when the production is limited but they just happen to have one in the storeroom that a deal has recently fallen through on. Being aware of your limitations may not mean that you will be upgrading to the 'premium' package, but you will be in a better position should unforeseen circumstances mean extra expenditure is required from your monthly budget. Your car breaking down is a prime example.

Anyone familiar with Murphy's Law would know the saying, 'Anything that can go wrong, will go wrong'. This isn't a doomsday saying, it is simply a warning to expect the best but plan for the worst.

Needs versus wants

A lot of sales processes exploit the fact that we are creatures of emotion. We have a wide range of emotions and any number of them can override the power of rational thought. A good salesperson can incite excitement in the customer and have them sign the contract of sale on just about anything before the customer's rational mind kicks in. With the wide variety of financing programs, customers can sign up to a contract that locks them into the sale whether it suits them or not. This is where a distinction has to be drawn between what we *need* and what we *want*. This will help you to avoid situations of buyer's remorse or unnecessary drains on your cash flow.

Distinguishing the difference between what you need and what you may want will change your whole life. 'Needs' and 'wants' are two very different thought processes, and the way you justify purchases has a huge impact on your budgeting and spending.

The basic human needs include:

- shelter

- food

- water

- air

- sleep

- sex.

What other needs do you have that you can add to the list?

....

....

It is easy to become dazzled by the beautiful people, bright images, high-energy music and other emotion-tugging marketing techniques used to sell products. Separating the logical mind from the emotional mind when it comes to purchasing items or services will help you to avoid becoming a financial statistic. Learning to ask yourself the question 'Do you need that or do you want it?' every time you are making a purchasing decision will help you to separate your emotions from your logical mind so that you can make the best decision.

Asking others the question will mean that they will encounter some conflict in their mind. They may have had their heart set on the purchase, but logically it may not have made much sense. You will see the realisation on their face as they snap out of the emotional spell. Salespeople don't like it when you pull the rug out from underneath a potential sale, but your friend or family member will be very appreciative.

Humans are brilliant electrochemical machines, possibly the most marvellous things on this earth. You can manage your electrical/chemical responses and impulses with clear and objective thinking, or you can let the responses control you. Eating chocolate creates an automatic chemical reaction in the brain akin to sexual pleasure. So, too, does buying wonderful new things. You need to be in control of that particular electrochemical process if your financial situation is going to improve.

Asking the question 'Do you need that or want it?' will interrupt that automatic response of pleasure. You will rationalise things a lot better and you will find it easier to distinguish the difference between your needs and wants.

We will all have different triggers and reactions, but simply asking the 'need versus want' question will always bring you back to a level playing field and empower you to make the best decision.

Do you really *need* that top-of-the-line plasma TV/pair of Jimmy Choos/brand-new car or do you *want* it?

....

....

Apart from shopping, can you list three other occasions where you could use the 'need versus want' question?

....

....

....

A lot of people want to keep up with the Joneses, but I met them the other day and they were looking very tired and worn out from trying to stay ahead of everyone else. They keep fighting about money, too.

Managers' debt syndrome

After my car accident I found full-time employment in a sales position. My usual 38-hour week included some overtime, so I made an average wage after the tax man had his share. Within a short time it became my responsibility to look after the shop and manage the day-to-day operations of the business.

I bought a great car and took out a personal loan to pay for half of it. The loan was easily arranged because it could be 'serviced' with my wage, and the bank took ownership of the vehicle as security. I signed the paperwork so that the racing car look-alike with the huge wheels and body kit would be mine, and I drove it around with pride. I thought people might be looking at me and wondering what I did for a job. I could see them admiring my car and enjoyed thinking that they might want one, too. My ego was fuelled by this car and it made me feel good to drive it around.

My sales job gave me a condition that I have named managers' debt syndrome (MDS). It's the 'want' that people get when they receive a pay raise or promotion and feel that with the new level of responsibility comes an image that has to be displayed and maintained. This may mean buying or upgrading to a 'manager's' style of car or house to let everyone know that you have made it. MDS will tell everyone that you are successful, but the reality is that you have most likely increased your debt levels and liabilities simply to appear richer.

The level of MDS is generally proportional to the amount you earn. I've coached a lawyer who earned in excess of $150 000 per year who still had trouble servicing her debt. She lived in a big house and drove an expensive car, but as the old saying goes, 'The bigger they are the harder they fall'. While the houses, clothes, toys and cars get bigger and more expensive with the increased wage, so too does the liability of leveraging a comfortable stress-free life against potential disaster. The habits and behaviours behind the misuse of credit remain the same no matter what amount of money people earn.

At the time I bought my car I also had a credit card and a personal loan that had been used to purchase some equipment and toys. My personal budget was shot from my own case of MDS. On close examination I was chained to my work for seven years just to pay my debts. Any money earned that didn't go towards my immediate living costs (which were high due to my car) went straight to the bank. This meant more than just working in the same place for seven years, it meant that I had no real chance of investing for the future or being able to take advantage of any opportunities that came my way. I was trapped and living on limited time.

Does this sound familiar?

Are you working for the bank instead of working for yourself?

Are you happy with your current financial position?

I'm guessing you're not if you're reading this and there is something that you want to change. What would you like to change?

....

....

If you had absolutely no limitations on resources, what would you change about your life right now?

What in your present life resembles your ideal life?

....

....

What are you happy with in your life?

....

....

What is happening now or what are you doing right that is working for you?

....

....

How does that make you feel?

....

....

What are you doing or what beliefs do you have that are already moving you towards your goals?

....

....

Have these questions helped to clarify what you need to be focusing on?

....

....

If not, what else can you do? Who can you ask for assistance?

....

....

Making your current actions and the actions required clear (and in your own words) will help you to move forward at a better pace. We're surrounded by answers, we just need to discover what the question is and ask it.

When you realise how serious the situation is and what it means to your life, you will gain motivation to step up and make the changes you need to get ahead.

Types of debt

There are two types of debt. The first type is used as financial leverage to give you a leg up in business or investing and is known as 'good' debt. The costs of using this type of debt are offset by taxation benefits and profit margins. The second type of debt is used for personal purchases and is known as 'bad debt'. The interest and fees cannot be claimed against taxable income as a deduction. Bad debt is used to purchase items such as cars, furniture, hi-fi systems and televisions, which drop in value as soon as they leave the store.

Using credit cards or store cards to make your purchases, and then not paying those cards off while still in the interest-free period is bad debt. Buying personal items that you can't afford and paying for them over a period of months or years along with interest and possibly fees and charges is also a bad use of debt. Put simply, bad debt takes money out of your pocket, whereas good debt puts money in your pocket.

For example, if you purchase a car for $20 000 using personal finance, you can expect to pay $30 000 in repayments by the end of the loan. The effect of compounding interest over a few years and the tendency of people to pay only the minimum monthly payment means the lender can expect to make a tidy profit.

At the end of the five or seven years of the loan, if you still have that same car, it may be worth only $10 000 due to depreciation. Essentially, the debt alone has cost you $3000 per year and you have only an old car to show for it (that's before fuel, insurance, servicing and so on). It's an expensive way to buy a vehicle. How do you feel about your money going down the gurgler like that?

There are very few cars that increase in value. Contrary to popular belief, a car is not an asset. An asset puts money in your pocket, whereas a car takes money out of your pocket. A car is a liability.

What could you do with $3000 extra in your pocket each year?

How would you feel if you knew that you got out of bed each morning because you enjoyed your work, not because you had to make a car repayment that week?

Is your car a fashion accessory that is costing you too much?

Interest-free-period deals

'Buy now and pay later!' Sales and marketing tool or famous last words?

When I speak with people who have money the advice is unanimous. If they don't have the cash, they don't make the purchase. Sometimes when you are setting up a new home those 'interest-free' deals can seem like a godsend. Other times they are there so that you can upgrade from a standard television to a huge crystal-clear high-definition plasma variety. The salesperson invokes the buyer's emotions and applies an urgency technique such as, 'We don't have any more in stock because at this price they have run out the door, but we can box this one up for you if you like'.

When you use debt to purchase clothes, plasma TVs, sound systems and cars, you are buying items that decrease in value. They might make you look and feel good, but in reality they are lining you up against a wall with a blindfold on. It's money that you can never get back or claim for taxation purposes. Before these forms of credit became available people had to find alternative methods of furnishing their house or apartment.

Have you ever bought furniture or electrical goods on an interest-free term from a store? Did you budget for your repayments to be paid off before the end of the term? Did you read the fine print in the contract? If you are even a dollar short, the store may be able to charge you the full amount of interest as soon as the 'free' term has finished.

The interest begins calculating on the first day you make the purchase and may be a huge amount by the time the 48 months is over. I have heard of people paying $5000 for a lounge suite that was bought on sale for $1500. They missed their repayment deadline and the interest charges were added to the total.

The store makes its sale and either way the finance company makes its money. The application fee, monthly fees and any late fees are going to come in no matter what. The big money is when the account is unpaid (in part or in full) and the unsuspecting customer gets hit with the interest bill.

These interest-free deals can work well if you manage your budget correctly from the start of the arrangement; however, they can be incredibly cruel if you find your-self caught out. The agreements tend to be available only on purchases of more than $1000 and can stretch out to 1000 days. This might sound like a great offer— $1000 over 1000 days is $1 per day—but did you add in the application fee and the monthly accounting fee? What about an allowance for possible late charges for the months you are overwhelmed or forgetful? Perhaps you trusted the person writing the application to make the calculations for you and you trusted that they were correct.

As a former debt collector there were many times when I spoke to people who had been set up incorrectly and the mistake had compounded. Ultimately, it is up to you to ensure that the paperwork is correct.

The keys to avoiding the pitfalls of interest-free deals are:

- know your budget and don't overextend yourself

- read the fine print and be sure you understand the contract you are entering

- pay a deposit and then budget to pay the contract out early if you do decide to enter one.

If you can't afford a particular item right now, buy a similar item second-hand, put it on lay-by or save up for it. You will be much better off if you live within your means.

Remember, interest free is not 'free'. You still have to pay for the item within the allotted time frame, so be sure to work out your budget and stick to it.

Chapter 4

HOW DEBT WORKS

*The most powerful force in the universe
is compound interest.*

Albert Einstein

Credit is a tool of leverage that can work for us or against us. Now, we know that there's 'good' debt and 'bad' debt, but how does debt actually work?

Over the term of any loan the interest charged compounds. Understanding how compound interest works will give you the motivation to begin reducing your liabilities right away.

There are two types of compound interest:

- *negative compound interest*. This type works against you and takes money out of your pocket

- *positive compound interest.* This type works for you and puts money into your pocket.

There is nothing insidious about compound interest, nor is it a huge trade secret like so many 'investing' gimmicks make it out to be. When the power of compounding interest is backed up by regular savings deposits, an account can grow and work for you.

Watch a tree as it grows. As it takes in nutrients and sunshine, the number of leaves multiply and more branches grow to allow for more leaves. The root system expands to take in more nutrients to feed the larger tree. The tree is compounding its assets and growing at an ever multiplying rate.

I'm sure you have heard the statement 'interest is calculated daily but charged monthly', but have you seen it work and do you really understand what it does when it is working against you? The interest calculation curve for a loan is shown in the following diagram.

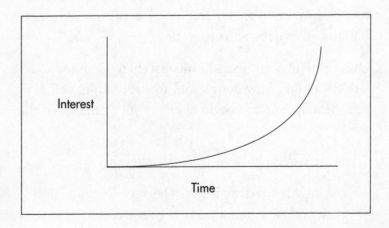

On the first day of the loan the interest is calculated on the principal and added to the amount you owe. On day two interest is calculated again on the previous day's total, which means that you now have interest being calculated on the amount that you borrowed *plus* the previous interest calculation.

I've tried to simplify the compound interest equation by setting it out in the following table.

Day	Amount to be repaid
1	Borrowed amount (Interest is calculated)
2	Borrowed amount + interest from day 1 (Interest is calculated)
3	Borrowed amount + interest from day 1 + interest from day 2 (Interest is calculated)
4	Borrowed amount + interest from day 1 + interest from day 2 + interest from day 3 (Interest is calculated)

And so it goes on. At the end of the month the interest is totalled and added to the amount that you owe.

You can see how the interest curve grows and becomes steeper and steeper in a short period of time. From day two you are paying interest on interest. What do you think that will that mean for a loan over the next 25 years?

When it comes to paying off the loan—for example, a personal loan or home loan—there is a pattern to the account balance, which is shown in the diagram overleaf.

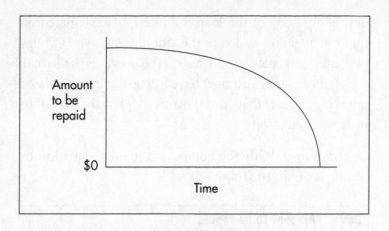

Initially the curve is flat. At this stage you are fighting against the power of the interest calculation. Very little progress is made as you make your regular payments and chip away at the principal amount that you borrowed. The best example of a debt curve is a home loan that has an extended term of more than 20 years.

It is only by about a third of the way through the term of the loan that you start to see a real reduction in the amount of the principal. This type of loan is known as an amortising loan — and no, it has nothing to do with love or lust, it simply refers to the way the debt is paid off.

The way credit agreements begin is key to financial institutions' profit margins. When a person signs the agreement to take out the loan the interest starts calculating from that day. For example, if the loan is for $100 000 at an interest rate of 8 per cent over 25 years, the balance of the loan by the time you make your first payment could be up to $100 666. If your minimum monthly payment is only $771, the balance of the loan will only be reduced by $105 or 0.1 per cent. The calculation for the interest curve for the next month will then begin at the balance of $99 895. The curve is shallow at the beginning, but gains momentum over time.

If the interest is charged monthly, then the amount of interest calculated over the 30 or so days will be added to the account on the designated day. A magnified view of the amortising debt curve is shown in the following diagram. As you can see, negative compounding interest makes money for others and keeps you working for them.

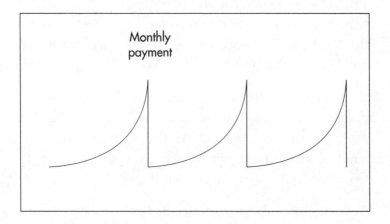

Add an account-keeping fee each month, miss a payment and get a late fee, and the amounts really start to add up. For example, if the account becomes delinquent (the bank's term for late in payments), then late fees are added and the compound interest curve that is already working against you starts to increase rapidly.

If you are behind on your payments, then the amount of interest calculated usually increases from the normal rate to what is generally known as a 'default rate'. If you don't bring your account into line quickly, the interest calculation curve can increase very quickly. The default interest rate is a penalty that applies to the amount of money over your limit and can be as much as 8 per cent or 9 per cent above your normal rate. I've personally seen a loan with an interest rate of 32 per cent. Can you imagine what the default interest rate would be on that account?

When you make a repayment (at the end of the cycle) the interest calculation curve stops and the cycle starts again. The amount that you have paid off the principal will lower the next starting point of the interest curve by that amount. The slope of the interest curve itself will also become shallower.

On a home loan this can be a very small amount (in the beginning), unless you are committed to reducing the principal and not just paying the minimum required amount each month. Every reduction counts and it's never too late to start saving your money.

By paying off only the interest, the balance stays close to the maximum for the first two or three years on a seven-year loan. When there is little movement you can see how this can be disheartening. The marketing of loan products is geared towards this disheartened feeling, so that a new finance company can win your business. Why not break the cycle?

Instead of being disheartened by looking at the balance of the loan and seeing it reduce only slightly, have a look at the amount of interest you are being charged. As you pay off your loan you will see that more of your money is going to pay the debt instead of going into the bank's pocket as interest payments. This is a simple change of focus but it's one that will better serve your interests.

Today we are surrounded by advertising that pushes products on us that we don't need but may want. Take the time to notice how many of these products come with interest-free terms or easy finance.

The marketing of home loans especially is buoyed by introductory offers, executive packages and any number of options that are designed to emphasise your negative feelings about the barely reducing balance or the poor performance of your current loan structure. A lot of people decide to refinance their home loan in the first few years when the curve is shallow because they see only small reductions in their balance. Their impatience is costing them dearly.

Here is a hypothetical situation for you. A person app-roaches you and offers you a choice of two options:

1   You can have $100 000 cash there and then, no tax or fees, and no waiting.

2   You can have a single cent immediately. This single cent must be placed in an account where the balance doubles in value every day for 30 days. One cent becomes two, then four, then eight and so on.

Which would you choose?

Although it's simplistic, the exercise will show you the power of compounding. The amounts are small at the beginning, but when the curve begins to create some real momentum the benefits you can gain through patience and persistence become clear.

Minimum monthly payments and direct debits

Have you had a close look at the wording on your bills lately? Have you noticed that the amount due is the minimum monthly payment (MMP)? While you're paying the MMP, lenders make a point of maximising their profits by offering direct debits. With a direct debit you don't have to worry about your MMP, it just comes straight out of your nominated account—which means you will be paying the maximum amount (to the cent) over the longest term. And the longer you are in debt, the better the profit margin for the bank, which means shareholders are happy and the CEO keeps his or her multimillion-dollar job.

Generally, a direct debit can be a good way to avoid getting late fees, but you will need to make arrangements to pay into the account in other ways, or arrange to increase the amount of your monthly direct debit to the nearest hundred. You can change your direct debit arrangement simply by filling in a request form with your lender. Rounding up your payment to the nearest hundred can be a great way to monitor your payments easily on your statement and the amount by which you reduce the principal.

A big problem I have with direct debits is that if the money is not in your account, you are likely to be stung with two fees—one for late payment from the business and one for the dishonour of the direct debit from your bank or financial institution.

Working as a debt collector I frequently saw this 'fee double-dipping' on customers' accounts. One small un-scrupulous loans company had tried five times in one day to direct debit a customer's account. That meant 10 separate fees in one eight-hour day.

Another issue with direct debits and MMPs is that a lot of loan consultants miscalculate the required minimum payment. Whether by a lack of education or thought, it is a problem that affects many customers.

In addition to forgetting to include the application fee in the calculation, many consultants take the amount owed and divide that by the term of the loan to arrive at an annual figure. From there they simply divide the annual amount by 12 to calculate a monthly figure. This system would work well if:

- each month had an equal number of days

- each month had the same starting day and date so that the weeks were in alignment

- there was an equal number of weeks in each month

- there were no leap years.

The inconsistent number of days and weeks over 12 months may mean that the account will fluctuate without you being aware. By the end of the year it should have corrected itself, but what if you had missed a payment or received a late fee because of one of the low cycles?

The small outstanding amounts from each month quietly accrue and can compound without you noticing until a debt collector informs you of the overdue amount. The customers in these cases are usually people who 'set and forget' their direct debits believing everything to be in order. The confusion and the fees can really add up if they are not corrected.

You need to be doing everything in your power to get ahead and pay off your debts early. To avoid the problems caused by MMPs round them up to the nearest hundred. By doing this you can be sure that your money will be going towards paying off the principal, and your debts will be paid out faster than you would have expected.

Why not pay a little more than the MMP? Or a lot more — how much can you afford? What is your maximum monthly payment?

How much better off will you be if you pay out a loan early?

....

....

Early payments

When drafting a loan document there is generally a time lag between when the loan commences and the date that the first payment is due. That first month is when you can wield the most power against the compounding interest curve.

Earlier in the chapter you saw what a standard amortising loan curve looks like. In the following diagram I have superimposed the same payment amount, but have made the payment well before the due date. You can see the instant impact on the principal amount and how you can reduce the interest payable on the account.

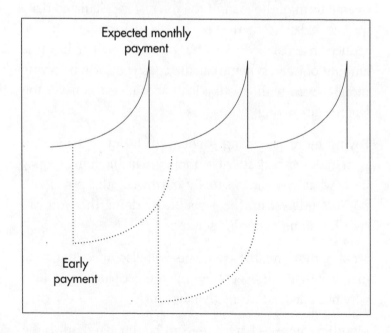

By paying ahead of the payment dates you can see how rapid progress can be made on a loan and the possibility of paying it off in half the time or less. Instead of being flat at the beginning, the curve can be placed in a downturn, which means you will wield more power over compound interest and more of your money will be going to pay the principal amount that was initially borrowed. Instead of waiting for the interest curve to mature you can cut it short. Even if you made an early payment only four times in the life of the loan, can you imagine how much you could save?

Paying early will stop the upward cycle of compound interest on the monthly calculation and will affect the overall term of the loan. If the interest is calculated daily on the balance, then every single day counts. If you reduce that balance, even by a little, it will reduce the amount of interest being calculated, so you will be saving money. Even with existing loan accounts it is never too late to start saving.

Paying more or paying sooner will mean that more of your hard-earned after-tax money will be going to pay back what you have actually borrowed (the principal), not just interest on the account. By doing this you can start reclaiming your life sooner.

Making more regular payments will also affect the cycle in a way that will benefit you. If you get paid fortnightly, why not make a fortnightly payment?

Monthly interest charges used to be the standard in the finance industry. When awareness grew that loans could be reduced rapidly by making more regular payments the financial institutions were quick to come up with a remedy for their profit margins. If a person applied for a home loan and stated that he or she wanted to make fortnightly payments, the financial institution placed a clause in the agreement that the interest would also be charged fortnightly. So although the compound interest curve was only half the height, there were now twice the number of interest calculations to make up for it. The amortising curve therefore remained the same and the person's power to get ahead actually reduced, because apart from making weekly payments it became difficult to short-cut the loan curve.

Is the loan facility that you organised to pay fortnightly charging you interest on a fortnightly basis? If so, it may worth seeking specific financial advice so that you can find a solution that will allow you to regain control of your finances and make the most of your available financial power.

A facility that may be available to you on your home loan is a 'repayment holiday'. If you're ahead with your payments, a repayment holiday allows you to take a break from making payments. This can be useful should you become sick or injured and can't work for a period of time. A repayment holiday should be treated as an emergency fund only and should be repaid if you dip into it, so that all of your previous hard work is not lost. Some personal loans also have this type of function.

Some home loans also have an option to redraw funds. This facility needs to be treated with respect. Personal loans tend not to have this function, but when you are ahead on the payments you may be contacted by your lending institution with an offer to let you use your accumulated funds.

For example, you may be sent a letter that says you have $1000 available and you can redraw it. This $1000 has been paid off early and has reduced their profit margin, so of course the lender will want to regain some of those losses rather than spend money on advertising to find a new client. The $1000 may seem tempting, because it's not every day you are offered that sort of money, but you have to remember how much it will cost you to pay it back.

Getting into the habit of dipping into the available funds on a regular basis will end up costing you more money unless you have the discipline to manage your spending habits 100 per cent of the time.

If you have an insurance policy on your home loan, check the terms. You may need to be out of work or incapacitated for six weeks before the policy kicks in and begins to cover you. The coverage may also be limited to a specific term such as six months. You can treat the repayment holiday or redraw facility as a back-up self-insurance policy. The extra money that you have paid into the loan is not just reducing the interest you pay, but is creating a buffer between what you are contracted to pay back and what you actually pay back. This gap can be used when you become sick or injured without any waiting. Workplace accidents or even simple accidents around the house or in the car are an unfortunate reality. This is a case of expecting the best but planning for the worst.

Generally, there are no forms to fill in, no claims managers to speak with, no waiting periods and no exclusions (which insurance companies are very good at). Your money is your insurance, so if you can create that buffer it can be put to good use should the need arise. I'm not saying that you should use these means to replace your insurance altogether, simply that getting ahead on your payments will give you more flexibility and power in your life.

Early repayments will result in your loan being paid out sooner than planned and you may be charged an early repayment fee. On one of the loans that I repaid early there was an early repayment fee of $100, which I would normally baulk at. However, I calculated that I would save almost $3200 on interest costs, so the $100 fee was a small price to pay.

Remember, looking at the big picture with loans and finance—and understanding how it all works—is very important.

Chapter 5

THE REAL COST OF DEBT

This would be a much better world if more married couples were as deeply in love as they are in debt.

Earl Wilson

When you're not aware of all of the implications of being in debt it's easy to be complacent and continue with the same program of behaviour. The impetus to take control of your finances and get out debt can only come when you understand what being in debt is really costing you—both in terms of your finances and your life.

How much are you really paying?

Have you ever considered how much money you will be repaying when you take out a loan?

Before I was educated in finance I actually believed that if I borrowed $10000 at 10 per cent (on a personal loan over seven years), I would pay back $11000 in total. However, the real cost would have been more like 140 per cent to 160 per cent of the $10000 I had originally borrowed, due to the compounding effect of interest and account fees. I would have been paying about an extra $4000 to $6000.

Of course, the shorter the loan term, the less power that compounding interest has. A five-year loan for the same amount will cost you less in interest than a seven-year loan.

Here is an exercise for you. Have a good look at the following ad and take note of how the information is delivered.

A little exercise in marketing

ABC Bank interest rate

9.29%

Comparison rate

10.35%

Warning: conditions and other things

Do you believe that this ad is showing the ABC Bank's rate compared with a similar loan offered down the road at XYZ Bank?

The interest rate is more than a full percentage point lower than the comparison rate — which do you think is the better deal?

If you answered 'the 9.29 per cent rate', that's okay — that's what I wanted you to think.

A loan is like a pie. The interest rate is one piece of the pie (it's a big bit but not the only one). The fees and charges are the other pieces. The entire pie is called the comparison rate. The ad is showing you the one loan from the one bank. The interest rate has been separated and highlighted to show you the individual components of the loan.

The ad has the low interest rate as the focus, making it larger and bolder. The actual total cost of that loan — the comparison rate — is also shown because it's required by law. To the uninitiated it may look like the 9.29 per cent loan is being compared to a 10.35 per cent loan, but the two figures are the same loan. The cost (the comparison rate) goes up by more than 1 per cent due to the fees and charges on that account.

When you take out a loan you need to look out for how much the credit is going to cost you. How many of your after-tax dollars is it going to take out of your pocket?

The comparison rate tells you what the loan will mostly cost, as it takes into account all of the fixed costs (interest, application fees, monthly fees and so on) associated with that particular product. (Variable costs, such as late fees and early payment fees, are not included in the comparison rate as they may not apply to everyone.)

In the US the comparison rate is called the 'annualised interest rate', which is self-explanatory. Whoever in Australia decided on the term 'comparison rate' has simply made things confusing for customers. Unless you know and understand the financial lingo it can be easy to misinterpret what is presented.

Here is another exercise for you.

A second exercise in marketing

ABC Bank interest rate
9.29%
Comparison rate
10.35%

Warning: conditions and other things

XYZ Bank interest rate
9.85%
Comparison rate
9.90%

Warning: conditions and other things

Which loan would you choose now and why?

This was a loaded question. If you chose the XYZ Bank loan with the lower comparison rate, then, yes, you will pay less over the term of the loan. However, you aren't going to be just paying the minimum monthly payments anymore. You also won't be paying on the due date; you will be finding ways to pay sooner and reduce the balance.

If you chose the ABC Bank loan, you would have a lower interest rate to battle against as you pay it off. It would depend on the fees and charges and how long you were planning to pay it off as to whether you would take the deal or not.

Planning for the future and understanding your position and payment ability will go a long way to helping you decide which loan to use. Getting the advice of a finance professional who can analyse your situation can be beneficial because he or she can help you to choose the right products for your needs and situation.

The fine print that goes with all offers of credit, such as those just shown, can be an entertaining read, listing all of the inclusions, exclusions, preclusions and conditions. A big poster advertising a low interest rate may get you in the door, but you may end up paying a higher rate because you don't fit the profile that was advertised. The term 'conditions apply' means that all sorts of parameters may change, and that your financial profile may not fit the perfect profile that the ad is pitched to.

There are finance companies that know that once you have been sitting in a salesperson's tiny office alone for what seems an eternity (while the salesperson checks the paperwork), you will agree to almost anything just to get the car, hi-fi system or television that you have your heart set on before anyone else snaps it up. So it's essential that you understand what you're signing up for and that you read the fine print at the end of any offer of credit.

Debt and relationships

Money and debt can ruin families and friendships. You may know of or have been directly affected by a situation where money has been borrowed and been only partly paid back or not paid back. This type of debt is quite common, with estimates placing private debt levels in the billions of dollars. This hidden hole in the economy is placing stress on personal relationships, as well as the hip pockets of many Australians and New Zealanders.

How many times has money created a problem in your life? Have you ever lent money to a friend and then had that friendship change as a result of the transaction? Have you ever borrowed money and then through some unfortunate set of circumstances been unable to pay back your debt?

Many of the issues that surface in these situations can be avoided, however. Some situations call for tactful resolution and at times the forgiving of a debt, especially to a family member. Sometimes there are situations where people continue to borrow money and place others into hardship. The legal system is full of cases that could have been avoided with some prudent planning and management at the beginning.

Loans between family and friends leads us to another area of hidden credit — STD (sexually transmitted debt). The typical STD starts when boy meets girl. Boy asks girl to co-sign the loan for a new car. A few years later the relationship goes bad and boy and girl break up. Boy starts defaulting on the loan payments and as girl guaranteed the loan she is left holding responsibility for the loan account. The credit agency then goes after the girl because her name is on the loan document. This type of situation can damage or remove someone's financial power and set them back years.

As with anything, prevention is better than cure. We would all like to be generous, but by protecting yourself with a written financial agreement you can avoid all of the bad feelings or problems if the relationship turns sour.

If your partner is not allowed to get a loan from a reputable agency, thus requiring you to co-sign for the loan, then most likely something has been picked up by the lender during the application process to give them fair reason to reject the loan. So be sure you know exactly what you're signing before you do so.

Private loans between family and friends can also result in angst and strained relationships. Engaging a lawyer to set up a financial agreement between the borrower and lender can seem costly. However, the cost could be far less than the stress and money involved if the situation goes wrong.

There is actually a do-it-yourself document for this very situation—the Australian IOU kit. Ten minutes of forward planning can save years of hardship. The IOU kit can be found at <www.ioukit.com.au>.

Know your limits

Have you ever been served a meal that tasted as great as it looked and you ended up eating too much? You wolf down the food without thinking about the consequences. Very soon the large plate that was overloaded is bare. You sit back in your chair and realise that your pants are feeling a bit tight, so you undo the top button. It's not long before you are feeling bloated, lethargic, nauseated and regretful.

Okay, that may be slightly over the top, but too many people are doing exactly the same thing with their finances. They aren't sitting back and truly assessing their capabilities before they jump in.

I've seen countless articles about brokers fudging figures to get borrowers over the line to be able to afford that loan on paper. How much do you think this hurts people in the long run? To the broker or loan agent it may be the difference between a sale and them not making a bonus that month, so be aware of motives when signing those pieces of paper and authorisation forms.

Before signing a loan agreement you should always:

- read the fine print and ask questions

- take responsibility for yourself and your actions.

Sure the house or holiday is exactly what you have been dreaming about, but can you really afford it just yet? Keep in mind that circumstances can and will change. Every day items and services increase in price and interest rates may rise. Within six months the price of fuel can rise by 20 per cent, but does your pay cheque also go up?

You're better off working on the safe side of your budget than being on the edge. Give yourself a buffer. You need to be able to service your loans easily, as well as cover all of your living costs. Too many people are going out and financing themselves to the hilt just because they want it and can 'afford' it now.

I'm constantly hearing the comment: 'All I saw was a shiny new car. I didn't care about what the interest rate was and what the fees were. I was just hoping the bank would approve my loan'.

Remember, we are very emotional creatures. Advertising and sales are geared towards manipulating emotions. Marketing companies are very aware of what makes people 'tick'—and therefore what will make them buy. There always seems to be someone else interested, a short-time-only offer, one left in stock and all of the other lines salespeople use to invoke a sense of urgency to make you buy it now.

When I go to buy anything I've learnt to allow myself a couple of days to rationalise the purchase. If the item is still there and I still need it (not just 'want' it), then I go ahead and buy it, but you need to know when to walk away from the deal.

Some time ago I flew a private plane for a company in Papua New Guinea. On one occasion I was approached by the owner of the company and some friends of his to organise a fishing trip. The plane was fuelled, the flight plan was completed and all of the other preparations had been made at my end. I had advised the passengers of their baggage allowances, as aircraft have special design limitations and have to be operated correctly. Exceeding the limitations will cause the plane to fly in a manner other than normal and can result in an accident. Going beyond the limits is not only foolish, it's also illegal.

Although they had been advised of the baggage allowances, the passengers insisted that they bring more luggage. Now, I could have overloaded the plane and I might have gotten away with it, but it would have pushed me beyond my limits. Once you get away with something it's too easy to try it again.

I refused the extra baggage and received a written warning for my actions, but I believe that my safety, integrity and reputation were worth it. In the end the owner and his friends decided to go via one of the ships they had.

It's the same with your finances — know your limitations and stick to them.

Chapter 6

TAKING ACTION

To will is to select a goal, determine a course of action
that will bring one to that goal, and then hold to that
action till the goal is reached. The key is action.

Michael Hanson

Frenchman Michel Lotito is documented as having con-
sumed an entire Cessna aeroplane over two years and
holds the Guinness World Record for the strangest diet.
The way he did it was one bite at a time.

I'm not going to ask you to go down to your local airfield
and start chewing on the tyre of an aeroplane, but rather to
take small consistent bites out of your debt levels in order
to pay them off. It will take consistency, determination,
self-belief and discipline on your part. As you get used
to this new program of behaviour and start realising the

benefits, you can take bigger bites out of your liabilities. There are different ways of reducing debt and I will take you through some of them in this chapter.

The power of belief

Picturing yourself at the finish line and brandishing the trophy is very important in the process of training your subconscious mind to work with you to achieve your goals.

If you want to get out of debt and improve your life, but inside you have a voice of doubt or disbelief, then your subconscious and conscious mind are in conflict. You want to take action, but have trouble starting or get sidetracked by trivial things. This conflict can mean that you may not absorb or use the information that can be of real benefit to you until you free yourself of these limiting beliefs by deleting, substituting or changing them altogether.

It may take some time and effort, but you can reprogram your brain. You can program yourself for success. The way you talk to yourself, your inner dialogue, will play an important part in your success.

What do you tell yourself on a regular basis?

....

....

Do you tell yourself that you are no good with finances or money?

....

....

Do you berate yourself for not being able to save and letting all of your money slip through your fingers?

....

....

Do you tell yourself that you have the power to achieve anything?

....

....

Do you hold yourself in high regard?

....

....

What beliefs could be limiting or stopping you from forging ahead?

....

....

Do you believe you are worth more financially than you are actually getting paid now?

....

....

If you speak to yourself in a self-defeating manner, then the results will be self-defeating. Your brain will believe what you tell it and will make what you say come true. Put past failures or problems aside. By treating yourself with respect, using positive language and believing in yourself, you can turn your situation around.

I perform juggling workshops with my clients as a way to prove that they can do anything. If you look at someone successfully juggling three balls and think 'I could never do that!', this automatically places you on a course that will not produce favourable results.

The first thing I do is get the participant to say that he or she can do it. Just saying the words is not enough, however, because you can say anything. If you don't believe the words coming out of your mouth, there is nothing you can do to convince your brain otherwise. If you have any doubt in your mind, then there's little chance you will be able to beat the blockage and achieve success.

My clients don't just have to convince me, they have to convince themselves that they can juggle. This can be difficult, so the process I employ is one of gradual change and small moves. I get the participant to throw one ball correctly and when he or she performs that simple action correctly we move on to the next.

From an emotional standpoint each small gain shows on the person's face. A smile appears and a nervous laugh turns into a heartier, more genuine laugh. With laughter comes a release in the body's tension levels, as well as a release in the mind. When it becomes fun and the person can see that he or she is making progress the results come a lot faster. Usually within minutes I can have people juggling. What was once blocked in their mind by the language they used and any doubts they had has now become a talent they can practise and even teach someone else.

You might be unsure of the journey to come, but I'm sure that when you get a taste of victory and celebrate paying off your first debt, you'll be hungry for more. Share your success and excitement with the people around you—their support will encourage you further.

You really can do anything if you put your mind to it. One thing we can truly control in our lives is our thoughts.

In my years of fitness training I have seen that what you eat and how much you consume is very important in successfully managing your body. Like our bodies, our minds are extremely important and need a managed, balanced diet if we are to get ahead.

What are you feeding your brain with on a daily basis? What sort of exercise is it getting?

Is it time to take a break from feeding on a diet of doubt and disbelief?

Make your subconscious mind your greatest ally instead of a foe.

How do you get out of debt?

I'm the sort of person who will dismantle a machine to find out how it works. Understanding the principles and simplifying the inner workings of something makes it transparent. Gaining an understanding of the principles behind finance, debt and money in general will show you how the system works and how it is either working for you or against you.

When I eventually understood the system I realised how hard I was working for little or no gain. I felt as though I was trying to run up a slope covered with ice. No matter how rapidly I moved my legs I wasn't getting anywhere, and if I slowed down or stopped, I would slide down the slope into the abyss.

Do you feel as though you are in a similar position?

In the years after my car accident I worked full time, with 25 per cent of my monthly wage going towards my debts. I had a $10 000 car loan, a $5000 personal loan and a credit card that was maxed out at $5000.

The car and personal loan could have been paid off within seven years, but it would have meant working hard during that time to maintain the loan payments. I was overcome by my desire for more.

The other 75 per cent of my wage went towards my everyday living expenses. I had to budget for groceries, rent and my mobile phone, as well as pay electricity, gas, car registration and insurance, petrol, gym membership, house insurance and so on.

My cash was running out—fast! In fact there was no money left to have a good time with. I believe that life is about having a good time, not just working. Wouldn't you agree?

There were times when I couldn't go out with my friends because I simply couldn't afford to. I was embarrassed to admit to them that I had no spending money so I would say I was sick. During those few years I have never been more stressed or physically ill in my entire life. Just by repeatedly voicing out loud that I was ill caused my mind and body to believe what I said and actually to become sick.

Living within the finance cycle means your life is constantly spent playing catch-up. The average wage earner has to work for about three months of the year just to be able to pay the interest bills on their credit card. When you realise how much hard work you have to do and how potentially dangerous this is you will look for a better way.

Being in debt can be 'potentially dangerous' because not only do you have to ensure your health is up to scratch, but you have to remain employed to keep the money coming in. I remember a particular few weeks I decided to continue working when I had pneumonia. I had fainted at work on a couple of occasions and I should have been at home in bed or in hospital where they could monitor my lungs, but instead I was stressed about making the rent and car repayments that week. I had to work because I couldn't afford to fall behind the proverbial eight ball.

It was when I finally became free from debt that I realised I wasn't just behind the eight ball—I was at the point where I had to run around the financial pool table with my pants around my ankles. It's a funny way to end a game of pool if you lose, but it's motivation enough to at least get one ball into a pocket no matter who you are playing.

Being in debt is like playing a game and losing continuously. Have you heard the saying, 'It's not whether you win or lose. It's how you play the game that counts'?

If you are using credit cards, personal loans, car loans and so on, you are playing a losing game. We find ways to justify these things to ourselves and trick our minds into continuing with the same old practices. People may comment about the clothes and cars, and the recognition alone makes us feel good. It may be hurting us financially, but the good feelings created by the compliments and the attention are what reinforce the use of credit to buy all of the latest must-have items.

Take a minute now to imagine how good you will feel and how many people will compliment you on how refreshed you look when you aren't stressed and worried about getting up to go to work just so that you can make a credit card payment.

Will your brow be furrowed with worry?

Will you have more time for others in your life?

Will you feel more relaxed?

Will you be able to get out and do more of the things you enjoy doing?

Seven years is a huge chunk of a person's working life if they're only working to pay off debts. Sure your purchases may give you a bit of pleasure initially, but there is a lot of underlying pain that you will just be trying to cover up for the rest of the term.

It's the financial institutions' business to make money, so they find the best ways to get as much of our cash as they can. But it's your life, isn't it? Why can't you just reclaim it?

Ask yourself the following question out loud: 'How can I become debt free and enjoy myself so that I can make the gains in life that I need, want and deserve?'

What can you do?

I realised that my fancy car was keeping me in trouble. At $10 000 it was only a relatively small loan, as I had paid a substantial deposit when I bought the car, but it still put a dent in my pocket of $260 each month.

My $5000 personal loan had me paying another $140 per month and my credit card was an extra $100 per month. It was a tough decision, but I sold my car for $15 000 and was able to pay out the two big loans. The car is used as security for a 'car' loan, so you have to be able to pay the secured loan out in full. The bank will get very upset if you sell its car and don't hand over its money.

I bought myself an old Alfa Romeo that had rust in the bottom of the doors and a broken seat, but it had a solid engine and running gear, which got me around reliably, although not in the style I was used to. That little silver car performed the job of getting me from A to B while I concentrated on paying off the last $5000 owed on my credit card and then saving for a new car.

I realised that with a runabout type of car more money would be saved than before and my cash flow would heal quite quickly. My car insurance went from $650 to $150 per year, which was a saving of $40 per month. The car didn't need to be professionally cleaned, which meant $10 was saved and 30 minutes of my life was recovered for more fun each fortnight.

The vehicle registration cost was cheaper because of the transfer from a six-cylinder to a four-cylinder car. My fuel bill went down by half to only $30 per week, and my stress level went down as I didn't have to worry about the car getting dents and scratches.

On one occasion my cool red car was 'keyed' and the whole car had to be repainted. I was without transport for two weeks and the insurance excess was hefty. Sure the loan could be serviced, but the extra stress of having to find the $600 excess payment was the turning point when I began to wonder if owning that vehicle was really worth it.

The person who keyed my car actually did me a favour by helping me to realise the true costs of my money management. Selling my car was a hit to my pride, but the massive changes in my life were worth it.

I started to reclaim my life, as well as regain control of where my money went. I discovered that I was able to focus on more important things than just going to work to pay bills. It was a time to regain who I was and to take the chance to make some improvements.

I had an easy out by selling my car, but what have you got sitting around your place that you don't use or is a bit excessive?

Do you have a four-wheel drive when you could be using a small car for the same purpose?

Do you have an expensive luxury car when something in a more moderate price bracket would be more suitable for your needs?

Do you have a set of golf clubs you don't use?

Could you own a part share in a boat or caravan instead of owning it by yourself?

Have you considered holding a garage sale? Perhaps you could combine the effort with your friends and neighbours.

Have you thought about giving an online auction site a go? You might be surprised what you have sitting around that others may want and be willing to pay cash for.

Are you renting a storage shed for possessions that aren't worth the rent you're paying?

Taking back control of your finances doesn't just involve selling things to pay off your debts. There are other things you can do.

Do you have a qualification that you aren't using?

Are you in a job where you could be getting paid more?

How long has it been since you asked for a raise? (Check the wording of your terms of employment first in case asking for a raise gets you into trouble.)

I know a second job may not be an option (especially if you have family), but if you're in dire need to reduce your debt faster then it's worth considering. If you have children, can you take on some babysitting or minding of other people's kids for a few hours each week?

Look at all areas in your life to find where you can cut back. Some of the things we spend our money on can really blow your mind when you line them up side by side.

How often do you buy cans of soft drink and snacks from a vending machine or takeaway coffee and sandwiches?

How soon could you be debt free if you put that money to work and packed your own lunch each day?

Are you an impulsive shopper? Do you go out for groceries and come back with the latest gadgets or fashions?

Do you drink alcohol on a regular basis? Do you need to have a drink in your hand to have a good time?

Does that cigarette really help to control your stress? Are you aware that by stopping smoking you could potentially channel $3500 into paying off your debts each year? When your financial obligations are paid out that $3500 could be put towards an annual holiday.

Do you like to play the pokies?

I often hear people talk about the wins they make playing the poker machines, but not one can provide an answer when I ask them how much money they put in to make a 'win'.

Gambling legislation in Australia states that average payouts are in the order of 86 per cent, but have you ever looked at the auditing counters on the machines? Next time you're at a pokie lounge have a look for the small counters—they're usually on the side of the machine. See how much money has gone into that machine in its life and you will also see how much it has paid out. The payout figure will be closer to 60 per cent.

The temptation to recycle any small wins is quite high, with the average punter putting their hope on the 'big win'. One machine can have had millions of dollars put through it. Each club has at least 40 machines and there are hundreds, if not thousands, of clubs in every state and territory. Hoping for a win on the poker machines or lotto is not going to get you out of debt.

Is there someone you can talk to or ask for help with your smoking, drinking or gambling?

It's never too late to get help and there are people out there who will listen. It may just take a bit of encouragement to pick up the phone or talk to a trusted family member or friend.

There are plenty of alternative sources of entertainment and activities you can do that make you feel good without losing vast amounts of money or taking risks with your next mortgage payment. Have you considered:

- going to the movies?

- seeing a play?

- visiting family or friends?

- joining a social club?

- volunteering for a good cause?

- inviting your friends around for a meal?

My hope is that you will trade in your old habits for new ones that will make you feel good, as well as be good for you and for the people around you. You never know, you might even find a new addiction to the gym or a passion for walking along the beach.

What would you like to get out and do?

What activities do you enjoy?

What makes you happy?

List some of the things that you will do to start bringing your finances under control. Do your best to list four items.

....

....

....

....

When you create your budget, give yourself some play money. This is cash you can blow while having fun. Go skydiving or partying with it—just go out and enjoy yourself. Live your life to the fullest.

It is the best thing in the world to have goals that you can strive for and achieve, but you have to remember the journey. Take the time to look around and enjoy the sights and sounds.

If you make your new life a chore, you will find that you'll go back to your old ways and you'll be in a whole world of pain again. You will be comfortable with the old ways, though, because you've been there before. It's amazing what living conditions we can become accustomed to. Don't fall back into the old program!

Legalised slavery?

After I sold my car I realised that I had claimed back about $400 per month. Instead of channelling this money into my lifestyle or savings, I put it to work paying off my credit card. I could have earned 5 per cent or 8 per cent by putting my money into an interest-bearing savings account, but by reducing the balance of my credit card I was essentially gaining a 20 per cent return. I went from working for the bank to having them work for me—well, almost.

When I walked into my local branch with a bank cheque to pay out two of my loans, the teller with whom I was familiar said something to me that made the entire situation sink in: 'You still have your credit card, so we still own you!' It may have been in jest but it opened my eyes to the world of credit and lending.

When I coach people through their financial issues the teller's words ring in my ears. Although they are legitimate businesses, the financial institutions run them well and take no prisoners. There may be leniency here and there, as well as a few educational programs, but when push comes to shove they will move in and foreclose.

By signing loan agreements we make ourselves slaves to the system, and we can only end the term of slavery by buying our way out. In his time Abraham Lincoln ended one form of slavery, but it continues today in a different form. Own your own life!

Understanding bankruptcy

To a lot of people declaring bankruptcy seems like the only way out of debt, or a way to avoid paying accounts whether or not they are insolvent. This is an unfortunate belief as bankruptcy can create all sorts of problems further down the track. Declaring bankruptcy should only ever be the final step when all other avenues have been exhausted and there is no other way to manage the situation.

In Australia there are two levels of administered debt recovery, and they are part of the Bankruptcy Act. A Part IX debt agreement is available only to people who are insolvent. It allows the person in debt to create a plan in partnership with his or her creditors in order to pay off the debt without creating hardship. Financial hardship is generally defined as when a person cannot pay for food, transport or essential services. A Part IX agreement means that any interest on the account is frozen. Any fees or other charges cannot be applied, which will make the debt easier to be cleared.

It is a way for you to work out with your creditors how best to settle your debts without becoming bankrupt. Failing to comply with or maintain a Part IX agreement may be grounds for a creditor to move the account towards a Part X agreement or bankruptcy. Bear in mind, however, that creditors don't have to agree to the repayment plan in the first place and can ask you to declare yourself bankrupt or they can have you made bankrupt.

Another option is to voluntarily declare bankruptcy. A Part X agreement does not exempt you from paying the debt. If you earn above a pre-determined threshold your income will be garnished to pay the creditors. The application can be done through the Insolvency and Trustee Service Australia (ITSA). On application for bankruptcy your assets will be assessed by the trustee of the account and may be sold to cover the debts. In this situation your house can be sold or any assets that aren't considered 'personal' by the trustee can be liquidated to cover the debt. Some people have found that by selling their house or major asset to a friend for a low nominal amount they can have the sale process reversed by the trustee in order to recover the correct amount of money.

The problem with declaring bankruptcy is that it generally lasts for three years. In this time your credit options can be limited and you must disclose to any potential creditors that you are currently bankrupt. This can make it difficult to apply for something as simple as a mobile phone account. You may also have to hand in your passport to the trustee of the account, so any overseas travel will be out of the question. You will have to apply to the trustee to regain it.

Add to the financial problems the associated social stigma of being referred to as a 'bankrupt'. Children whose parents are bankrupt can be bullied at school on account of that fact, and friends and family who don't understand the situation can shun bankrupts for fear of catching some sort of unseen disease or virus. The impact and implications of bankruptcy have a wide reach.

Once discharged from bankruptcy the matter is not over as you will be listed on a register, which is a matter of public record. This can mean that any application for credit or security in the future may be subject to extra scrutiny. In short, declaring bankruptcy should be the last thing you would want to do.

For more information about Part IX and Part X agreements, and voluntary bankruptcy, visit <www.itsa.gov.au>. Information on bankruptcy legislation and the options available in New Zealand can be found at the Insolvency and Trustee Service website, <www.insolvency.govt.nz>.

If you think you need a helping hand to point you in the right direction, call your local council office or social support group and ask them about financial counselling services in your neighbourhood. These services are usually free.

Snowballing

It's time now to take a look at a proven debt-reduction strategy I call 'snowballing'. This strategy is about using the power of momentum. Watch a snowball as it rolls down a hill. It picks up speed and grows larger the further it travels. This method of debt reduction works on the same principles, hence the name.

I will show you how snowballing works using an example. Joanne was a client of mine. She owned a country property and had a number of debts—for feed, water deliveries, horse agistment and transport, and a couple of delinquent telephone bills. Joanne had eight debts altogether and had started to receive those nasty letters with the stickers in dangerously bright colours.

Fortunately for Joanne she had some disposable income and was willing to make the necessary lifestyle changes to pay off her debts before the debt collectors came calling. Together we created a budget for her. This helped Joanne to see where she was overspending and how she could channel her available funds to cover her liabilities. She managed to set aside $800 each month, and made arrangements with each of the creditors to pay $100 off each debt each month.

Don't be afraid to contact companies or people to whom you owe money to set up a plan. It is in their interest to help you, so they should work with you to achieve a positive result. Most businesses I know would rather see the cash trickle in until the debt is paid completely than to see nothing at all.

Some people say that you should target the debt with the highest interest rate first to save some money. That's okay, but it isn't going to make much of a difference in the outcome unless your level of allocated income to pay off your debts will mean that your plan will take more than a year to show some real results.

Snowballing allows you to knock off the smaller debts first and gives a cause to celebrate while building up to the point where you smash the last and largest of the debts, a real cause to celebrate. As each debt is paid out, the money that was allocated to that account is then directed to the next smallest account. The power of the snowball gradually becomes larger.

It's important to start something new with small manageable steps. Have some fun and enjoy your victories no matter how small they are. Every step you take is another step closer to your success. Snowballing allows you to celebrate paying off your first account in a relatively short period of time.

Joanne was fortunate that she could spare $800 per month. Even if you are not in the same position, you will find your financial situation improving as you begin to pay off each debt. Joanne discovered she was spending money on the wrong things at a time when she needed to be focusing on getting rid of her debts. Retail therapy was Joanne's vice — buying new clothes and shoes made her feel good.

After assessing her situation she realised she could easily attain positive results in a short period of time using the snowballing method. The celebrations after extinguishing each debt made it fun for Joanne and helped to reinforce the new program of behaviour.

What are you doing with your money at the moment that may be making you feel good temporarily, but doesn't resolve the underlying problems?

....

....

Where will you be in one year if you continue with the same spending patterns?

....

....

How good will you feel and how much lighter will your burden be when your debts are gone forever?

....

....

Your conscience can be cleared, your credit report fixed and your stress levels will reduce markedly.

If you make an arrangement like this, be sure it is within your budget and be sure to pay when you say you will. There's nothing as damaging as a broken promise.

Joanne's progress can be seen in the table opposite. Within three months debt four was gone. Joanne then allocated the money she had been putting towards that debt to the next lowest debt, which was debt eight. She was able to assign $200 per month to pay it off.

The amount being put towards the lowest debt keeps getting bigger as each debt is paid off, so that eventually all of the debts are paid out. Can you see how Joanne's snowball is getting bigger and how much potential it has as it charges down the mountain?

One of the great things about this method is that almost all of the debts are paid out before the final expected payment. How impressed will your creditors be when you pay out your debts before the due date you give them?

Joanne could have refinanced, but it would have cost her an application fee and essentially made a ninth bill. Eight small hurdles would have become one giant one.

Debt	Amount due	Amount due end month 1	Amount due end month 2	Amount due end month 3	Amount due end month 4	Amount due end month 5	Amount due end month 6	Amount due end month 7	Amount due end month 8	Amount due end month 9
1	$3000	$2900	$2800	$2700	$2600	$2500	$2400	$2300	$2200	$1900
2	$1000	$900	$800	$700	$600	$500	$400	-	-	
3	$1500	$1400	$1300	$1200	$1100	$1000	$900	$800	$500	-
4	$250	$150	$50	-	-	-	-	-	-	-
5	$750	$650	$550	$450	$350	$100	-	-	-	-
6	$1200	$1100	$1000	$900	$800	$700	$600	$400	-	-
7	$800	$700	$600	$500	$400	$300	-	-	-	-
8	$600	$500	$400	$250	$50	-	-	-	-	-

Would you rather run a race with a few small hurdles to jump over or run the same race with a 10-metre-tall brick wall in your way?

It took discipline, hard work, sacrifice and a word of encouragement every now and then, but Joanne was able to overcome her financial problems. By the time she got rid of the last debt she had settled into a comfortable lifestyle for her income and suddenly had an extra $800 each month to play with. To celebrate being debt free I bought her a book on investing.

Take a moment right now to picture yourself when you pay off that last debt and feel the weight lift from your shoulders.

How light do you think you will feel?

Will you feel like dancing on the spot?

Will your smile be one of the biggest and most genuine smiles you have worn in a while?

Will you jump up and punch the air while shouting 'Yahoo!'?

Start taking action right now.

Chapter 7

BREAKING YOUR CREDIT ADDICTION

Remember that credit is money.

Benjamin Franklin

When the GFC hit in 2008 the money dried up. Banks started making it harder to obtain finance. One thing that did keep coming were invitations in the mail to sign up for a great new credit card that offered a low interest rate or none at all if you just transferred all of your debt onto it.

It is these offers of easy credit that have put the world in the position it is today. The warning signs of the GFC that couldn't be brighter if they tried still have not deterred people from using credit. Of all the personal finance products offered by financial instutions the credit card produces the best return when it comes to fees and charges.

A credit card can be a fantastic tool of convenience as long as the balance is paid in full before the interest begins to accrue. As a 'revolving' source of credit it can be easy to ignore their bite when you become used to them. But they can be vicious little blighters if you don't attend to them. A credit card is like a leech—it stays on you and quietly sucks blood that could be used elsewhere.

There are several problems with credit cards as I see it:

- For every $1000 you have on the balance it costs you at least $20 per month in interest.

- Credit card marketing is quite competitive with many cards boasting 'up to 55 days interest free'. The key words here are 'up to'. It depends when you make the purchase and when your interest is calculated for the month. There is no automatic 55 days interest free on all purchases.

- The minimum monthly payment that appears on your bill each month is usually only 2 per cent of the balance (after interest has been calculated and added for the month).

- Fees and charges are put straight onto your balance and can therefore push you over your limit if you're near it.

- They are too easy to get and too easy to use.

- Every now and then we get offers to increase the level of our available credit, which often simply results in higher debt levels.

- Balance rollover offers with low interest rate cards are tempting, but can land you in real trouble because the first card is generally never cancelled, so you can end up with two maxed-out credit cards instead of one.

- Cash advances on credit cards are expensive. Interest is charged immediately, usually a much higher rate, and an additional fee is charged to withdraw the cash.

In the following pages I'll show you how credit cards work, and how to change your thinking and break your addiction to them.

Credit cards and minimum monthly payments

I hope you haven't gotten into the habit of paying only the minimum monthly payment to keep the wolves at bay. If the payment is 2 per cent of the balance, then there is practically no way you will ever pay it off.

Something that commonly happens is that people max out their card, but then only pay the minimum required amount each month instead of paying off the entire bill. I refer to people who do this as 'skimmers'. Skimming is an expensive way to operate.

If there's $5000 worth of credit on the card, the MMP will be about $100. That $100 is usually treated like a regular monthly bill, as shown in the following diagram. After one year the $5000 balance is still there, but the person has paid about $1200 in interest.

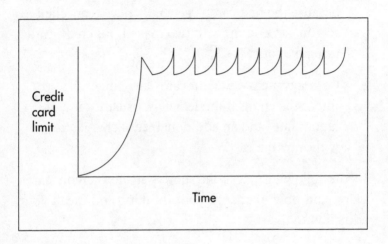

Is only paying the MMP something you are currently doing?

Have you just accepted that $100 bill each month as another everyday cost such as a phone bill?

How much do you take home after tax and how do you feel about that $1200 interest bill?

....

....

What action can you take today to start paying off your credit card?

....

....

What could you do with that extra $100 each month?

....

....

To some people that $100 might not seem like much, but let's look at it in a different way. What if I was to come to your house each month and ask for $100? I'm not going to mow your lawn, clean your house or cook any meals; I just want my $100. There's no way you would give me the money—you would most likely set the dogs on me! Take this chance to create a payment plan to get rid of that card.

When I worked as a debt collector I often encountered clients who maintained their credit cards at the upper end of the allowable limit. One client had a card that he maintained at its $6000 limit. He believed that keeping the balance just below the limit (at about $5970) would keep the account going with no problems.

However, not only was the account accruing monthly interest of about $150, but as soon as the interest charge was added it pushed the balance over the limit, which meant he then had the added misfortune of an additional

$30 over-limit fee each month. He not only had to work to pay the $1440 interest bill each year, but an extra amount of time to cover the $360 in fines.

The fines are like speeding fines—you're meant to associate painful thoughts with getting them, which should be enough for you to change your payment structure and your behaviour.

He continued to pay only the MMP shown on the statement and didn't check for any problems. The misunderstanding and mismanagement had cost him dearly over a long period of time. Thankfully, I was able to show him where he was going wrong and assist him in adjusting his payment structure and attitude to credit card payments.

That $30 fee could be used to buy a meal or a few cheap DVDs each month. I'd rather invest in my down time or a cash-management account than give it away.

Where are you giving money away unnecessarily?

....

....

The best way to rectify the problem forever is to pay the credit card off, and then pay the balance in full every month if you continue to use it.

Along with interest and other possible fees, there is the annual card fee, which drains money from people who have even the best of habits. About half of the bank's total profit comes from fees and charges, so change your behaviour and take back control of your hard-earned cash.

Someone else I have coached had a financial problem that is quite common in today's credit marketplace. Kate had a credit card that was almost maxed out. She was on a good wage and was able to service a second card, so she thought it prudent to apply for a new card and transfer the balance of her old card. She had seen television advertisements for 0 per cent interest rates for the first 12 months with a particular credit card. The 0 per cent interest rate sounded like a good chance for her to start making payments to reduce the balance of her existing account.

While this offer sounds great, the danger is the card you leave behind. Using a credit card to pay off another credit card is like using petrol to put out a fire. The old card should be cancelled, but more often than not it is left active and open to temptation. Sometimes only a partial balance transfer is available, so both cards remain active.

Kate applied for the new card and three weeks later the balance of the old card was transferred to the new one, which was then maxed out. The problem was she didn't cancel the now-empty old card. By thinking that the new card would solve her problems and not attending fully to her credit-use behaviour or adjusting her budget, Kate soon found that both of her credit cards were full and she had twice the problem. The solution Kate came up with? Another 0 per cent introductory rate credit card to try again.

You can guess what happened next—yes, three maxed-out cards and debt levels spiralling way out of control. Even with 0 per cent interest rates the level of debt became overwhelming. Sure she could service the cards, but just paying the minimum monthly payment was not going to get rid of the problem.

By the time Kate sought professional help her 12-month grace on interest payments had expired—the mounting interest bills had prompted her to take action. She took out a $30 000 personal loan to cover the credit card debt, which allowed her to pay out the account over a period of five years with a regular payment plan. In the previous chapter I demonstrated how to pay off debts without consolidating, but in Kate's case she needed the discipline of the loan structure, as well as the reduced comparison rate it offered, to adjust her payment structure.

By employing techniques such as fortnightly payments and early payments where possible, including depositing her tax refund cheque and any windfalls, Kate was able to significantly reduce the balance of her loan well ahead of the normal debt curve. Now all of the cards are gone and Kate is on the right track to paying off her debt.

The problem that exists now for Kate is that she's cash-flow poor. She has to work for a couple of years to pay this debt off and can't take advantage of any opportunities or investments that may come her way in that time. Kate wants to buy a house, but has to wait until she reduces her loan liabilities.

In 2007 the Census figures for Australia showed that we are spending on average 114 per cent of our wages. If I spend 100 per cent of the cash in my pocket, then all of my money is gone. How can people spend 114 per cent?

How long do you think that sort of spending can be sustained before total financial collapse and bankruptcy?

How long can you afford to be out of work before you are in trouble financially? Two weeks? Three weeks?

It's too easy to look at the credit you have available and see it as spending money. You need to shift your focus and see only the cash in your pocket as your spending money and your credit card as something you have to pay off as soon as you can. A credit card is only a convenient tool in a cashless society, for paying bills over the phone or shopping online.

A debt-friendly tool that credit companies have introduced is the debit card. It works like a credit card, but uses your own money instead of someone else's. It may be worth investigating with your financial institution.

Credit limit increases

A lot of people treat the offer of a credit limit increase as a pay raise or free money. Suddenly it's a chance to go out shopping because you have an extra $3000 available on the card. And it will only cost you an extra $60 per month. That's affordable — isn't it? It's all too easy; it's all too tempting.

Credit limit increases are treated as a reward for people who pay their bills on time and who have not reached or gone over their limit too often. If you've 'been good' (and paid lots of interest in the past), you are allowed to increase the amount you can borrow.

With a limit increase the principal debt increases and becomes harder to pay off unless you are lucky enough to come into some money; for example, through an inheritance, a lottery win or a huge tax refund. But how often can you bank on that happening?

Take some action today to start paying off these expensive debts. Put the money you would normally spend on lottery tickets to paying off your debts and credit cards. There's a guaranteed win if ever I saw one.

My own credit card limit went from $3000 to $6000, then $9000 and finally $14000. When maxed out, a $14000 card can cost you $3500 per year or more. You can end up paying far more for an item than you would have if you paid cash for it.

It's time now for a reality check on your credit cards. What is your credit card or store card currently costing you per year?

$_____ (monthly interest) × 12

= $_____

Do the sales and specials seem so special now?

If you have more than one card, you must do the sums for each. You need to see how much these things are really costing you.

As you progress with paying off your cards you can decrease the available credit limit on each card to reduce the temptation of reusing them.

Serviceability

I touched on the topic of serviceability or how much you can afford to pay earlier in the book. Serviceability is a term financial institutions use to describe your ability to pay back what you have borrowed plus the interest and fees.

When applying for a loan the loans officer will always ask you for some basic information about your budget. Do you know what your real day-to-day costs are? If you completed the budget in chapter 1, then you should be well aware of your position.

I love renovating houses and when I draw up a budget for a job I make sure that I multiply my final calculation by three. For some reason the renovations usually cost three times what I expect them to. There is always something that 'pops up'.

If the loans officers multiplied the basic calculations on their customers' budgets by three, then it would be a more realistic figure. However, if that was the case, then none of us would get a loan approved for anything. Why then do so many people give only minimum figures when asked about their personal budget?

It's always good practice to factor some contingency money into your budget. You never know when the fence will fall over, the car will blow up, the water heater will require replacing and so on. I don't want to sound like a doomsayer, but these things need to be considered and accounted for.

Applications for credit should allow you to live comfortably with no disruptions in your day-to-day life, but are you really able to?

How much are you hurting at the moment because of your debts? Are you able to service them comfortably?

....

....

If not, what action can you take to fix that?

....

....

There is a solution to every problem. The key is not to focus on the problem, but look beyond it to the solution and ask questions. Good objective questioning on your part will help the solution become clearer.

Closing accounts

When you close a credit card or loan account make sure that you have paid it out in full. Interest is calculated daily, so paying the balance from a statement you have received in the mail may mean that the account remains open due to that extra interest that has accumulated. You will already be behind the eight ball because of the time that it takes for the statement to reach your letterbox and then for you to pay the account. This small amount, if left unattended, can attract late fees and interest, and all sorts of trouble can ensue.

When closing accounts:

- always ask for a current payout figure

- be sure to pay the account before or on the day stated, not one day late

- always confirm with a company representative that the account has been properly closed and request a letter from them as evidence

- cut up the credit card and deposit the pieces with the bank or financial institution so that they can assure its destruction

- celebrate your new-found freedom and be proud of your achievement.

One of the calls I made when I was a debt collector was to a customer whose account had accrued massive late fees and was seriously delinquent. The customer was furious, but after chatting with him for a while I found out that he had originally paid what was written on the statement that was sent to him. That sounds fair, doesn't it?

His statement was processed on the fifth of the month and initially he had only $10 left to pay. The statement arrived in the mail on the 13th and it stated that he had until the 23rd to pay the $10.

When he went to the bank on the 22nd to pay the account it had quietly accrued more interest since the fifth. He was unaware of this extra interest and just paid the $10, believing the account to then be closed. However, the figure on his statement was not a payout figure and was subject to change.

A couple of months went past and he threw the bank's subsequent mail in the bin thinking it was advertising. However, in those two to three months there was a small balance that kept the card active and in that time he had accrued an annual fee, multiple late fees and interest on those fees. His non-payment of the account was picked up by the computer, which had then put him into the debt collection agency database.

In the following months he was contacted repeatedly by debt collectors who without any apparent explanation demanded that he pay the money. These were calls he just hung up on. By the time the account came to me it had reached more than $600 in fees and default interest.

The problem was not only painful and stressful for him, but it was almost at the point where it would have been written off by the bank and sold to an external collections agency, which would have resulted in a black mark on his credit report. A non-payment notice on your credit history can affect the possibility of future investment or business loans and personal finance. If you're interested in receiving a copy of your credit history, visit <www.mycreditfile.com.au>.

Ignorance of the problem is no excuse as ultimately we all have to be responsible for our own actions, whether we like the consequences or not. In the end the customer came to an arrangement with the bank and paid out the account.

If you have a problem with an account, it is better to continue paying the account and bring it out of danger. When your problem is resolved and if the bank is wrong, it will credit your account with what you are owed. Don't allow the fees to get out of control and put you in a worse position.

Making a stand or protesting to a computer is not going to solve the problem. Rather, it may further compound the problem and increase your stress levels. If you notice something incorrect or that you don't understand on your statement or bill, then it is always wise to get straight on the phone and have a company representative explain it to you. Don't wait and don't think that your question is too stupid. The biggest waste in this world is a question left unasked.

Chapter 8

THE TROUBLE WITH REFINANCING

The only man who sticks closer to you in adversity than a friend is a creditor.

Author unknown

A home is something that should increase in value over time and provide you with shelter and good memories. However, a big problem is that more and more people with personal debt think it's okay to put the balance of a personal loan or credit card into their home loan to take advantage of the lower interest rate.

The popularity of this debt-reduction strategy goes back to our education (mostly through advertising campaigns) about looking at interest rates only, not at what it will really cost us in the long run and if we can no longer make the required payments.

We are actively encouraged to put personal debt on our home loans by the marketing of finance products. There are advertisements on television that show testimonials from people who say they have 'saved' more than $1000 each month simply by refinancing. Sure, they may have reduced their outgoings initially, but they will be hurting more in the long term and losing more money to the power of compounding interest.

Do you think that the advertising and encouragement is there to help us get out of debt or for the financial institutions to generate a profit by gaining new customers?

If you don't have the discipline or cash flow to make the extra payments required when borrowing against the equity in your home, then leave your home out of the equation. Set up a dedicated savings account. It may take you a few years to save up, but to put it in perspective at least you won't be paying the holiday or furniture off for the rest of your life. In fact, you'll have the power of positive compounding interest working for you to help you reach your goal faster.

Once you're back in control of your finances and have cleared all your debts, using the equity that you have available in your home loan can be a great way to get started with an investment portfolio. There are a number of tax benefits to using your home as leverage for investing; however, you will need to do your research and contact a competent and qualified financial adviser to help work out the best plan for you.

You are risking a lot when you consolidate personal debt into your home loan, more than just paying too much of your hard-earned income over a long period of time. The home loan is a secured loan, which has your house as collateral. This means that the financial institution owns your home and lets you live in it while paying for it, sort of a reverse lay-by. If you default on enough payments, then the bank can and will send in the sheriff to reclaim its property.

A lot of money is written off by financial institutions because they can't recoup the costs even if they do re-possess a car or boat. These items lose value as soon as they are bought, and as a result the value is just not there to cover what has been borrowed. In my time as a debt collector the bank I worked for had a yard full of cars of the same model it couldn't sell because there was no market for them.

A house, however, increases in value and is a lot easier to sell. No business likes to write off or lose money as it has a negative impact on the profit margin, so finding ways to secure their bottom line is imperative to maintaining maximum returns for shareholders and/or stakeholders.

How mortgage brokers are paid

There are a couple of different ways mortgage brokers make money. The lender pays the broker a 'finders fee', which is usually a percentage of the amount that you borrow. The more money you borrow, the higher the commission the broker gets. These types of commissions don't come out of your pocket.

Another type of income mortgage brokers receive from your home loan account is what is known as a 'trailing commission'. This payment continues for the life of the loan, and is meant to cover the cost of the broker providing ongoing service to the borrower.

Every time you make a monthly payment on your home loan, a payment is made to your broker from the lender, this may also be a percentage of the balance of the loan amount. It's only a small figure, but multiply that by a thousand customers or more and the monthly income for the brokerage can be massive. Is your broker providing any information or services to assist you in reducing your debt? If not, contact your broker and ask what he or she can do for you.

As you pay your home loan off and the balance decreases, the monthly trail commission becomes less. This may mean that the broker will have to go out and drum up some new business to maintain or increase his or her income. It is easier and costs a business less to keep an existing customer than it is to get a new one.

Consequently, you may be encouraged to transfer your personal loan into a home loan structure. When you consolidate your personal loan or credit card debt into your home loan the mortgage broker receives an increased trail commission on that increased amount.

Do you think that some of the loans brokers may have, or may develop, an unhealthy interest in keeping your loan balance at its highest amount?

Do you think that having a large balance and topping it up with personal debt on a regular basis is doing you a favour?

There are some dodgy brokers out there, and since the deregulation of the home loans industry many new mortgage brokers have sprung up, so a bit of due diligence on your part is required. I even know of some brokers who will put you into an incorrect loan structure for your needs just so that they can ensure a regular income for themselves. Ask plenty of questions and find someone who will work with you and who you feel you can trust. When you do set up a home loan structure, make sure it suits your needs now and for the future.

Some brokers return part of these commissions to their customers or to charities, which can be a great way to attract customers and keep existing clients. As always, however, it's important to make sure that the finance structure and product a broker recommends is suitable to your needs.

Refinancing: friend or foe?

To receive any benefits from refinancing it will depend on your individual situation and how you are working your finances. Yes, refinancing may improve your cash flow in the short term, but it's the longer term you need to consider. Refinancing puts you right back at the start of the debt curve where suddenly most of your money is going to paying interest instead of the principal. If you are just paying the minimum monthly payment, then you are costing yourself the most money.

It seems as though a lot of people are looking at the balance on their loan accounts and on seeing little or no movement are deciding to take their business elsewhere, somewhere they are promised a 'better deal' or a 'honeymoon interest rate'. They are refinancing based on offers made by banks or brokers that advertise low 'honeymoon' rates or other gimmicks designed to gain your business.

The problems with changing structures are the cancellation fees and establishment costs of setting up the new loan. Any progress that was made on reducing the original balance is lost as the time clock is reset to start another term (a 20- to 30-year period if you're using a standard home loan).

Check the figures on a home loan at 8 per cent over 30 years—there is a real chance that the cost is about 300 per cent of what you initially borrowed, which is a lot of dough out of your pocket. Do you think that the advertisements would be as appealing if they said, 'You can have your dream home today if you just agree to pay 300 per cent of what is advertised here!'

Do you really want to start the 30 years again when you have already made progress on your current account?

A little exercise for homeowners

To find out how much you will have repaid in total, multiply your monthly mortgage payment by 12 (to establish your yearly payment), and then by the term of the loan, usually 30 years.

Monthly payment × 12 = $_____

Yearly payment _____ × the term of the loan
= $_____

How much did you initially borrow? _____

See how much you're paying for your house now? Can you see the power of compounding interest?

Imagine how much the house would cost you if you had a 45- or 90-year loan? If you have or are planning to have children, what sort of legacy would you like to leave them?

When people refinance their home loan they tend to add the credit card debt, personal loans and car loans they have accumulated. For a personal loan (over five to seven years) you generally repay 140 per cent to 160 per cent of what you borrowed. If you were to put a $10 000 personal debt into your home loan when you consolidate, your monthly payments won't be as much, but you will actually repay about 300 per cent of what you borrowed. Your $10 000 loan will cost you an extra $15 000 of your hard-earned after-tax income. So you've lowered your required payments, but increased the term of your personal loan by an extra 20 or so years.

Is the extra cash in your pocket now (by reducing your required payment) worth it when you will be paying back far more than you initially borrowed?

How do you feel about that $10 000 holiday costing $16 000 if you use a personal loan, compared with costing you $30 000 if you use the equity in your home (if you just make the minimum requested payments)?

Is it really responsible to work your finances that way?

How many hours would you have to work to pay back $30 000 in after-tax dollars?

If you're working an average 38-hour week, then the amount of money that you can earn in a lifetime is finite, it's limited. It's time to take responsibility for how you spend it or you'll end up with little or nothing for the times and things that really matter.

What do you think about your $20 000 car costing you $50 000 or $60 000 if you use the equity in your home to purchase it?

How good would it be if you had an investment that returned profits to you each year that meant you could take a holiday or buy a new car regularly without having to take a cent out of your pocket? Could that be another goal for you?

It is possible to put personal debt into a home loan (to perhaps take advantage of a lower interest rate and costs or simplify your banking), but you have to be extremely disciplined to make the extra payments. You can't simply pay the minimum monthly payment. The personal debt portion of the home loan should be treated separately and paid off within three to five years.

In fact, putting personal debt into a home loan is certainly *not* something I would recommend, given the temptation of humans to push boundaries. It is within the realms of science and exploration to go a bit further, but to do so with your finances is foolhardy.

Chapter 9

YOUR FUTURE

The trouble is, if you don't risk anything,
you risk even more.

Erica Jong

Throughout this book I have shared with you knowledge that will assist you in your efforts to get rid of your debt. Now it's time for you to take control—eliminate the old program of behaviour and begin a new, empowering program. In this chapter we will look at your future and point you in a new and exciting direction.

Decision making

Positive decision making is a skill you should practise daily. Even the choice to let someone else decide is a decision that you make, it's just not an empowering one for you.

The best decision-making lesson for me was during my time in Papua New Guinea. I was piloting a Cessna 206 —a six-seat, single-engine utility plane—which was the perfect vehicle for learning how to fly in the mountains. The performance and safety of the small plane give it an edge over smaller Cessna models that are more widely used for training. Papua New Guinea is an area of extremely unforgiving terrain with mountain ranges rising suddenly to 5000 metres and deep valleys that provide the only options for small planes to navigate across the country.

I'd landed at an airstrip beside a small village called Tapini, which is nestled in among the mountains about an hour north-west of the capital Port Moresby. The Tapini airstrip is basically a grassy version of the ski jumps you see at the Winter Olympics. The end of the runway turns up and then drops 150 metres to the valley floor below. Directly opposite the end of the runway is the valley wall of a mountain range.

Sitting at the controls of a single-engine plane at the top of that steep slope is the most daunting and humbling experience a pilot can encounter. I remember staring down the mountain and across the valley to the grassed wall that faced me as I listened intently for the engine to make the correct noises in preparation for take-off.

Various scenarios ran through my head: what if the engine fails? What if there is a sudden gust of wind? What if someone runs across the airstrip?

Asking 'what if' can be debilitating. If I had listened to my fears, I would now be a permanent resident of the village of Tapini and I would certainly not be writing this book. Sometimes you just need to have a little faith that if you do take that big step in life, everything will be okay. As Susan Jeffers puts it in her book, 'feel the fear and do it anyway'.

Once you commit to the take-off there is no out, there is no maybe. You either go or you don't. Today I present you with a similar situation. You can stay where you are and continue down the same track with your finances or you can have faith in yourself and your abilities and make a decision to really go for it (and act on it) to change your life.

This is a Go or No-Go situation—you're in command and you need to make a command decision. What's it going to be?

What of the future?

How much more could you do in your life if you had an extra $400 each month in your pocket like I did after I sold my car? How would you get your money working for you to make even more?

The answer is investing. There's nothing scary about investing, it's just another type of education. Once you know how to invest properly the rewards and challenges can be quite fun and can give you a real sense of achievement. There is plenty of information on investing available in bookstores and via other sources that can help you to find your feet and take the plunge.

Investments come in all sorts of shapes and sizes, so there should be something that will suit your tastes and needs. Researching as much as you can will take some of the fear away, but the only real education will come when you jump in and start doing it.

If you know someone who has invested successfully, why don't you make a time to talk to them about how they did it? You can learn a lot by talking to others. They will most likely have made mistakes that they can help you to avoid.

Successful people take pleasure in helping others to succeed. A good mentor can help you achieve your own success far sooner and more easily than you expected.

There are plenty of share trading and real estate scams, but once properly educated you will be able to see them coming and avoid them. There's a massive difference between 'get rich quick' and actual success. Generally, higher risk means higher returns, while lower risk means lower returns.

As long as you do something that you are comfortable with you should see a benefit. If high-risk investments mean you are under unnecessary stress, then they may not be for you.

If an investment opportunity sounds too good to be true, then a bit of research or outside professional help (if necessary) will show you that the opportunity is most likely too good to be true. If you pay $100 or $200 for good independent advice and it saves you from losing thousands of dollars in a possible scam (or poor investment), then the advice is worth every cent. That was a lesson I learnt the hard way. A get-rich-quick investment once cost me thousands of dollars. Consequently I now work closely with my financial adviser.

Doing your homework on investments and other opportunities is a great way to protect yourself. You'll be able to step up and realise a great opportunity when it crosses your path and you may even be able to create your own through a business, concept or idea. This is where you need to find an investment vehicle that you can be comfortable with.

Investing wisely is like buying a second-hand car. You can purchase a great, reliable car if you know the car already or you're mechanically inclined. The other option is to have the car checked by a professional who can give you a report on the health of the vehicle. From that background research you can then make the decision to either buy the car or walk away from it.

Investing is like anything else you will experience in your life that is new. With education, application and practise it will become easier.

Have you ever wanted to invest in an existing business or create one of your own?

Do you have an idea that you would like to take out into the world?

Is there an opportunity to create a business in your local area?

Would you like to study at university to gain a degree or a particular qualification so that you can do something you really enjoy and get paid for doing it?

Would you like to invest in the stock market?

Do you enjoy renovating homes and working with your hands? Would you like to get started in residential or commercial property development?

If you can get paid or make money from doing something that you enjoy, then you will be streets ahead in the game of life. A good investment opportunity should be able to provide you with a vehicle to carry you into a positive future. By re-channelling the funds that had been going towards covering the costs of your debt, you'll find that your investment strength grows rapidly.

A life of abundance

Now may be a good time to start a new habit of helping others by dropping your small change into the collection tins for a charity that you believe in. Begin by getting rid of everything smaller than a 50 cent piece. I know how annoying those small coins are and you would be really amazed at how far each one will go.

If 1 per cent of Australians gave just five cents each to one charity, then $10 500 could be spent on finding a cure for a disease or helping people in need. That money would buy a lot of blankets for people without a roof over their heads in cold weather.

Knowing that you have helped someone else will make you feel really good inside, too. I know that I function better in life in general when I feel good. Giving money to a worthy cause not only helps others, it also teaches you that there is more than enough in your budget to go around.

When you feel as though you live a life of abundance your actions will reflect that. You will feel your confidence improve. You will find yourself starting to walk taller, smile more and greet strangers with a cheerful 'hello'.

What kind of world might that produce for you?

What effect do you think you might have on other people's lives?

What do you think a smile and a kind word will do for a stranger's day?

Like a magnet the positive energy I radiate when I'm feeling on top of the world seems to draw positive things and people to me. The whirlwind of positivity becomes almost self-perpetuating.

Throw all of your other coins in your sock drawer. You will be amazed at how much you have when you empty your sock drawer at Christmas time. Getting those coins out of your pockets, bags, purses and wallets can make life a little lighter, too.

The beginning of the end

The increased cash flow from getting rid of my own debts caused my eyes to open up on a brilliant world brimming over with opportunities and ideas. At the time I suddenly had $400 extra to spend and with the savings in other costs I ended up with an extra $650 to $700 per month in my pocket. It was money that I put towards investing.

I had stopped the powerful force of negative compound interest that had been working against me and turned it around so it began working in my favour.

My life still has its ups and downs, but it is much more fun and far less stressful than the constant battle to stay afloat. For me now the financial curve is not money that I have to pay back, but an investment that is growing in an account with my name on it.

I remember celebrating being debt free with fresh oysters at my favourite restaurant.

Now it's your turn.

Index

If you really enjoyed this book, please help us to help others by recommending it to a friend or family member.

Let us know your story.

Internet: <www.escapefromdebt.com.au>

Email: info@mpoweruaustralia.com.au

Subject: Escape from Debt